Praise for *The Law of*

D0595349

"This thoughtful book can supplement and en... ... ... a simple, new way to combine the Twelve Steps with novel techniques that encourage growth. Sherry Gaba has artfully crafted a method to transform your existence, offering a model for recovery that shows you how to be everything you ever hoped to be.

"In our work on VH1's *Celebrity Rehab*, I've seen the amazing connections Sherry makes with those who are so terribly disconnected from others and themselves. But you don't have to be a celebrity in recovery to benefit from her years of training and experience. Sherry provides a road map for rising above negativity and thinking of your self, your life, and your purpose in new and inspiring ways."

—**Drew Pinsky, M.D.**

"Sherry gives recovering people and their families a new look stemming from ancient times at a subject that's in the limelight again—how to stay sober and create as much joy as possible. Too many people are sober but haven't found the 'happy, joyous, and free' part. This book can assist you in that."

—**Melody Beattie**, author of *Codependent No More*

"Sherry Gaba has skillfully combined the solid approaches of Alcoholics Anonymous, current information from trauma literature, the ancient practices of mindfulness, and the wisdom and compassion gleaned from her years of personal and professional experience in *The Law of Sobriety*. She has created an effective approach and valuable tools for anyone beginning addictions recovery as well as for those celebrating years of sobriety and abstinence. *The Law of Sobriety* is a much-needed practical and solid addition to addiction literature."

—**Jane Middelton-Moz**, author of *Shame and Guilt: Masters of Disguise* and coauthor of *After the Tears: Helping Adult Children of Alcoholics Heal Their Childhood Trauma*

"Writing from the heart in a most readable style, Sherry Gaba guides readers in integrating the Law of Attraction and other universal principles into their recovery to deepen their sobriety in a holistic and out-of-the-box fashion. In following the Law of Sobriety, readers are guided to embrace an authentic life in recovery that is fully aligned to their true values, while embracing the power of gratitude, forgiveness, compassion, right action, awareness, and mindfulness. I highly recommend this book to anyone who yearns to experience the full joy of recovery, both newcomers and old-timers alike."

—**John Newport, Ph.D.**, author of *The Wellness-Recovery Connection*
and *The Wellness and Recovery Workbook Series*,
and senior principal, Wellness and Recovery Associates

"What happens when metaphysics meets Bill Wilson? You have this wonderful book. Sherry provides us with seven action-oriented suggestions to help us realize the full potential of our recovery. I highly recommend including this book in your recovery library."

—**Allen Berger, Ph.D.**, author of *12 Stupid Things That Mess Up Recovery* and *12 Smart Things to Do When the Booze and Drugs Are Gone.*

"*The Law of Sobriety* is a powerful and enlightened book for our times. With so much of society in the grip of addiction, Sherry Gaba's manual gives sobriety seekers all the wisdom of the spiritual, Law of Attraction, and Conscious Creation teachings crafted *specifically* to their experience and needs. It provides everything they need to help them right their lives and stay on the path of freedom from their addictions. No sobriety seeker should pass up this life-changing guide."

—**Jackie Lapin**, author of *The Art of Conscious Creation:
How You Can Transform the World*

"Sherry Gaba's book arrives at the perfect time! With the many struggles and challenges people are facing today, her fresh, out-of-the-box approach to addiction recovery revolutionizes how we view ourselves and offers us new gems of wisdom for creating more fulfilling and sober lives."

—**Steve Sisgold**, author of *What's Your Body Telling You?*

The Law of Sobriety

Attracting Positive
Energy for a
Powerful Recovery

Sherry Gaba, LCSW
As Seen on VH1's *Celebrity Rehab*

with Beth Adelman

Health Communications, Inc.
Deerfield Beach, Florida

www.hcibooks.com

The names, locations, and other identifying information of the individuals in this book have been changed to protect their privacy. This book contains general information and is not intended to be, nor should it be, used as a substitute for specific medical or psychological advice.

Library of Congress Cataloging-in-Publication Data

Gaba, Sherry.
    The law of sobriety : attracting positive energy for a powerful recovery / Sherry Gaba, with Beth Adelman.
        p. cm.
    Includes bibliographical references and index.
    ISBN-13: 978-0-7573-1515-2
    ISBN-10: 0-7573-1515-1
    1. Alcoholics—Rehabilitation. 2. New Thought. I. Adelman, Beth. II. Title.
HV5275.G33 2010
616.86'106—dc22

                                                                                      2010015708

Publisher: Health Communications, Inc.
        3201 S.W. 15th Street
        Deerfield Beach, FL 33442-8190

Cover photo by Christopher Glenn
Cover design by Larissa Hise Henoch
Interior design and formatting by Dawn Von Strolley Grove

This book is dedicated to everyone in recovery. You inspire me with your strength to live with purpose. I am moved by those who have found recovery and by those who return when they have lost their way.

Contents

Acknowledgments

I would like to acknowledge the most important people in my life, as well as others who have made this dream come true. To Scott, my husband, who has been through every step of this journey with me. You have watched me scream for joy in the wonderful times and have seen me in the most difficult times during this process of writing a book. You have been my inspiration every step of the way.

To my mom and dad, who never enabled me and allowed me to stand up on my own a very long time ago. Your support and love are immeasurable.

To my daughter, who is beautiful inside and out and who models everything a twenty-six-year-old adult woman can be. You are a hard worker and always go the extra mile. Thank you for being my daughter. I am a very lucky and blessed mother because of you.

I want to thank my editor, Candace Johnson, for believing in me and in the reason this book was published.

I wish to thank Beth Adelman for her contributions to this book, for making the process run so smoothly, and for keeping me very organized.

And finally, I want to thank Drew Pinsky, M.D., for having me as a guest on his radio show, *Dr. Drew Live*; for believing in me and inviting me to work with the patients on *Celebrity Rehab*; and for always getting back to me—even with his enormous schedule—as I went through this process.

Introduction

It was 1976. My parents had just dropped me off at my new home, the "party dorm" at San Diego State University. I was planning to study journalism. I hugged my mom and dad, said my good-byes, and in an instant I felt an overwhelming emptiness spread out from my chest until it was gnawing away at my whole body. It felt as if someone was stepping on me, preventing me from breathing. It was a familiar feeling. Throughout my life, I felt abandoned whenever I was left alone, even if it was just my parents going out on a Saturday night. I would cry hysterically while my brother just smiled and waved good-bye, so happy that they were leaving. I felt the same way when I went on a ski trip and my best friend canceled. I went anyway, but I felt empty and didn't really have any fun. Then there was the time I went to summer camp and cried myself to sleep every night, wishing I was home.

My problems may have started when I left the womb ten weeks premature. In 1959 they didn't allow mothers or fathers to have contact with their premature babies, so I spent my first two and a half months of life in an incubator. I was fed through needles that were inserted into my tiny feet, had an oxygen mask over my nose, and was hooked up to all sorts of machinery that kept me alive those two and a half months. I was not held or soothed by my mother—or anyone else. Now, as an adult and a therapist, I have learned that this is why I later had feelings of dread and insecurity when I felt alone or separated from those I loved. These feelings set me up for a future of bad relationships, settling for whoever would give me the attention I so desperately needed to fill that terrible void.

1

Attachment theory is a concept in psychology that says the earliest bonds children form with their caregivers can affect them all their lives. If basic bonding needs are not met early on, people often develop anxiety, depression, and a host of other problems. There is some evidence that this early developmental trauma can be triggered later in life if a person is affected by a situation that might reenact the experiences of those early years. Addicts and alcoholics often have a history of early developmental trauma, and an experience later in life may bring up old issues. Certainly, drinking and using drugs are ways to cope with issues of separation anxiety, social anxiety, trauma, or feelings of abandonment.

So there I was at college, going up in an elevator to the fourth floor where a meet-and-greet party was being held. I had never felt comfortable in groups of people I didn't know, so this party was definitely not my idea of a good time. But I was told it would be a great way to start meeting people in my new dorm. The elevator doors opened (in my mind, it felt as if this was happening in slow motion) and right in front of me were about fifty students talking, laughing, and seeming to be having the time of their lives. I walked out, and immediately a girl walked over to me, introduced herself, told me where she was from, and shared all the other small talk you have with a new friend. She took me over to the table where the alcohol was and asked if I wanted wine or beer. I chose the wine.

Nothing in my past had ever done for me what that first sip of wine did. I had one sip, then another, and my anxiety was gone, as if a gentle wave had just washed it away. I was more relaxed and social than I'd ever been before. I felt as if I could say anything to anyone in the room.

Finally, I'd lost that terrible insecurity I always had when I was among a group of strangers. I was home. This was the moment of relief I had craved my whole life. I realized that I wasn't alone but was part of something, and suddenly I was more comfortable in my own skin. That's what that first drink of wine did for me.

This liquid courage became my best friend during that year I went to college and lived in the dorm. I continued to use alcohol as a way to socialize, anesthetize my fears, and talk to others without feeling judged. I acted in ways that were completely not me; I did things that were entirely inappropriate and that I would never have dreamed of doing when I was sober. For many years, I told everyone I knew that they had to live away from home their first year of college. I would say, "It was the best year of my life."

It was only when I began to look at my substance abuse later on, when I was in my thirties, that I realized it was the alcohol that made the experience seem so enjoyable. When my mother came to visit me, my room was full of empty wine bottles that I was using as vases for dried flowers. She thought they looked "so cute," but that display was really a metaphor for what my first year of college was about: getting drunk nonstop.

My alcohol abuse subsided after that year. I went home for the summer and dropped out of college, so I guess I didn't need the wine as much. I gave up my dream of becoming the next Barbara Walters–type television news anchor and went to work as a secretary at a talent agency. Although I didn't drink the way I had in college, I serial dated as another way to fill up the empty space at my core.

I met my first husband at a nightclub called Le Hot Club and got married when I was twenty-two. We had a baby when I was twenty-five, and I got divorced at twenty-six. Despite the traumatic upheavals in my life, in all the years after college I drank very little. But ten years later, when I was in my thirties and trying to juggle single parenting, a career, going back to school, and a host of bad relationships, once again alcohol seemed to help me cope. I was so overwhelmed with all my responsibilities, all the losses from bad relationships, and all the feelings of being judged by mothers in two-parent families that I craved that wonderful wave of release alcohol offered. This was 1985, and there were not many single parents roaming the San Fernando Valley in California. It was a middle- and upper-class neighborhood, and there just weren't a lot of people I could relate to or who could relate to me. In fact, one of the reasons I went back to school at age thirty-five to become a therapist was to help other single parents. I have great compassion for single parents and always will.

I never drank every day, but when the weekend came and I had a date or was going out with girlfriends, the alcohol helped to take the edge off my anxiety. I didn't drink excessively, but even one glass of wine enabled me to just *breathe*. I couldn't have a good time without it.

I am not proud of my behavior during some of my drinking days. I am sure I embarrassed my daughter, my parents, my friends, my dates—but more important, I embarrassed myself. Do I feel some shame? Probably. Have I abused alcohol? Absolutely. There were definitely consequences to my alcoholic behavior.

It really doesn't matter to me what anyone else thinks about whether I am an alcoholic or just abused alcohol at certain times in my life. What does matter is that through my personal recovery program and my profession as a psychotherapist and a life coach, I have done a lot of work on discovering the hidden demons that caused me to use alcohol as a coping mechanism. Finally, I understood that I wasn't just drinking to feel good or to have a good time. I was drinking because that was my way to cope with my chronic feelings of emptiness and my inability to regulate my emotional pain and reconcile past traumas. What matters now is that I no longer use alcohol as a way to deal with life's stressors, difficult issues, or difficult people. I walk through my pain the best way I can, without the crutch of alcohol.

My own recovery was accomplished by finding Alcoholics Anonymous (AA). The program enabled me, for the first time, to not be a victim of my circumstances. I am so grateful to have found this twelve-step program, because not only did I find recovery, but I also met my husband at a meeting. I still go to meetings occasionally, and I recommend them to all my clients who are dealing with any type of addiction.

Twelve-Step Programs

Briefly, a twelve-step program is a set of guiding principles that outline a course of recovery from addiction. These steps include admitting that you have an addiction, recognizing a higher power that can give you strength, examining your past mistakes and making amends for them, and learning to live in a new way. Alcoholics Anonymous is the best-known twelve-step program, but there are several others. Most have some type of meeting, and sponsors who have been through the program help newcomers work through the twelve steps.

I have seen twelve-step programs work for countless people with addictions. But after ten years of helping others free themselves from a variety of addictions, I have come to believe that there are many roads to sobriety and healing the emotional wounds that have traumatized so many of my clients. I am a huge proponent of twelve-step programs, and they have become the accepted standard in addiction recovery, but they are not the only road to sobriety. Recovery is not a cookie-cutter process; each individual has to find what works for them.

Some people who walk through the doors of my office refuse to go to twelve-step meetings. Maybe they are afraid of opening up to others, afraid to admit they have a problem, or afraid they will be "found out" and possibly lose their job, relationship, or children. Maybe they don't believe in a higher power and the spiritual component turns them off. Some clearly don't understand that the program is about how to live life sober and not just about sharing stories of alcoholism or addiction. Should I tell them I can't work with them just because they don't want to go to twelve-step meetings? Absolutely not. I learned a very long time ago that you meet the clients where they are.

Because some people are so adamantly opposed to the twelve-step approach, I have had to take a hard look at how I can be of service to them, treat their addictions, and help them wrestle with their demons. I have realized that I need to meet them exactly where they are willing to be met, so they will keep coming to therapy and work on the issues that are holding them back from living a happy and purposeful life. When someone comes to me for help, it just doesn't make sense to drive them away because, for whatever reason, they cannot accept the conventions of a twelve-step program. My goal is not to lose them at our first meeting but to shed some light on their personal darkness, inspire them, and move them toward a transformative process.

As a psychotherapist, I am blessed to have the opportunity to work with addicts and alcoholics and watch them work through their resistance, pain, trauma, and, ultimately, their journey to recovery. Addictions and alcoholism have become the greatest part of my practice, although I also work with people struggling with depression, anxiety issues, the aftermath of trauma, problems encountered as a single parent, and self-defeating behaviors. In addition, I have worked with numerous clients as a life coach, watching them move forward in ways they had never thought possible in their careers, relationships, health, well-being, and spirituality. I have experienced real joy working as a life coach and psychotherapist on the television series *Celebrity Rehab 2, Celebrity Rehab 3,* and *Sober House,* as I watched the clients blossom through their recovery by taking baby steps toward living a more fulfilling and purposeful life.

I have a private practice and have also worked at various Malibu rehab treatment centers that cater to high-profile clients. A few years ago at one of these rehab centers, they showed a documentary film called *The Secret.* This 2006 film was executive produced by Rhonda Byrne, who also wrote a book of the same name. *The Secret* film and book introduce the Law of Attraction. As described in the film, the Law of Attraction says that feelings and thoughts can attract all kinds of events on a scale both cosmological and personal. In other words, people's thoughts actually control the reality of their lives, whether they realize it or not. (I'll explain this in much more detail in Chapter 1.)

When you visualize, you generate powerful thoughts and feelings of having it now. The Law of Attraction then returns that reality to you, just as you saw it in your mind.
—From *The Secret* by Rhonda Byrne

I noticed that after the clients watched the movie, the room became silent. They seemed to be inspired and said they felt glimmers of hope and even joy from the movie's uplifting message. They seemed to align with the concept of the Law of Attraction in a way nobody had expected. Over time, there was a change in the rehab facility. Clients who had been depressed, unmotivated, and detached became hopeful, inspired, and eager to work their sobriety program. They were ready to listen to what their counselors and therapists had to say in a way they hadn't been before.

Of course, not all the clients bought into the concept, and most of the clinicians thought it was nothing short of hocus-pocus. All I knew was that the clients were feeling excited about something. Their despair seemed to dissipate and they seemed to be encouraged to make changes and refocus on the things that were important to them. How could this be? How could a roomful of resistant addicts who lacked hope be transformed?

I must admit that when I first watched the movie, I, too, was moved. The skeptic and psychotherapist in me felt it was a bit too simplistic. And yet, I felt a surge of excitement motivating me to begin thinking positive thoughts. And as I thought about the Law of Attraction more and more, I realized the idea was not as far-fetched as it seemed.

One of the traditional therapeutic methods used in recovery is known as cognitive behavioral therapy (sometimes abbreviated as CBT). CBT teaches clients to reframe their negative thoughts into positive ones. Many addicts and alcoholics see themselves as inadequate, worthless, and incompetent. These thoughts develop early in their lives from a host of childhood experiences, and they become automatic. These negative automatic thoughts influence the way addicts view themselves and how they behave. The goal of CBT is to get the clients to turn these negative belief systems into more accurate, positive ones.

For example, often clients will tell me they are "unlovable" and "will never have a successful relationship." Notice the word "never." Alcoholics and addicts tend to think in absolutes—everything is black or white. It's my job to help them correct these distortions. In this example, instead of thinking they will never have a successful relationship, the idea can be restructured as, "The partners I attract while I am intoxicated are a result of poor choices due to my addictions; when I am sober, I will have the opportunity to choose healthier relationships." Changing the way they think about things opens up many positive possibilities in their lives.

This idea of reframing one's thinking coincides with the principles of the Law of Attraction, although the Law of Attraction takes a more mystical and purposeful approach. The Law of Attraction states that everything is made up of energy, including your thoughts. This means everything you think, believe, and feel will be attracted back to you. If you are feeling positive, you will attract positive feelings; if you are feeling negative, that, too, will be attracted back to you. CBT asks clients to reframe their negative thoughts so they can achieve a more positive outcome, while the Law of Attraction asserts that what you think, the universe will send back to you.

This concept holds hope for addicts who are struggling toward recovery but find traditional treatments are just not right for them. They come to realize that their repetitive, negative thoughts will continue unless they learn to replace them with more uplifting thoughts. And the Law of Attraction holds out the promise that positive thoughts will bring with them positive feelings and events. This is by far the easier way for addicts, who, for the most part, desire instant gratification.

Although the premise of the Law of Attraction is that what you think, you will manifest, the missing link is the action steps that must be taken to realize your dreams and desires. That's where this book comes in. It is a marriage of the Law of Attraction and the actions a person must take to recover from their addiction—whether the addiction is to drugs, alcohol, gambling, sex, shopping, nicotine, eating, or anything else. I call this marriage the Law of Sobriety.

This book is a how-to manual for applying the principles of the Law of Attraction and doing the basic work to live a more purposeful, meaningful, and addiction-free life. I believe there are many ways to get to sobriety, and the Law of Sobriety is one such path. Over the years I have learned that there is no single approach to sobriety. Surrendering to what works is how I work with my clients, and I have experienced firsthand an energy surge in clients who respond to the principles of the Law of Sobriety. If this book helps you transform your thought processes and brings you closer to the life you want to lead, I'm glad I wrote it!

ONE

The Law of Attraction and the Law of Sobriety

The Universe does indeed provide for your every need.
It is your feelings of fear and lack that get in the way
of simply allowing that to happen.
Trust is the answer to life's many questions.

—From *Choosing Joy, Creating Abundance*
by Ellen Peterson

The Law of Attraction has made a big splash recently in books, in seminars, and on talk shows. But what does it really mean? The Law of Attraction says the reality of our life is related to the thoughts—both conscious and unconscious—that we put out into the universe. Thoughts are a form of energy, and the energy we project into the world is the energy we will receive or attract back into our lives. Another way to put it is that whatever you direct your conscious attention to is exactly what will come about. The same holds true whether you focus on what you want in your life or what you don't want in your life; whatever it is will be attracted back to you. Therefore, it's important to be very clear in your own mind about what it is you desire and want to manifest in your life, because the universe is listening.

We attract back to ourselves whatever we put out into the universe on two levels: the energy of our emotions and the energy of our thoughts. For example, if you are emanating joy, peace, and happiness, you will attract those emotions back to yourself, and if you are projecting fear, rage, and discontent, that is what you will attract back. This is the emotional part of the Law of Attraction. When it comes to our thoughts, if you think you will never be able to achieve a goal—for example, getting the job you want—then you never will achieve it. But if you think you will get that great job, and you imagine yourself working there, eventually it will happen.

The proponents of the Law of Attraction say it works because all forms of matter and energy vibrate in a certain way and are attracted to other matter and energy vibrating in the same way. The general vibration of a person represents the balance of his or her thoughts. As we become aware of our thoughts, we can change our vibration by thinking things that are more in harmony with what we really want. When we learn how to consciously control what we think, we are no longer controlled by our own negativity or by ideas about ourselves that come from other people. We can then raise the level of thought at which we vibrate and attract happiness and serenity to ourselves.

It's not necessary to believe in the idea of a vibrating universe to make the Law of Attraction work for you. You can understand it literally (and many people do), or you can see it as a metaphor for understanding how we can all get trapped in negative ways of thinking and the damage that can do in our lives—and how changing our thinking can change our lives.

Positive Psychology

One idea inherent in the Law of Attraction is that people with a positive outlook tend to have happier lives, and psychologists agree. In fact, there is a whole branch of psychology that is known as positive psychology. Positive psychology is the scientific study of the strengths and virtues that enable individuals and communities to thrive, and the types of psychological interventions that build happiness. There is an International Positive Psychology Association, as well as positive psychology centers at the University of Pennsylvania, the University of Michigan, and other universities that promote research, training, and education about positive psychology.

Researchers in the field of positive psychology have found that the qualities recognized as character virtues and strengths seem to be fairly consistent throughout the world. The most commonly endorsed strengths that contribute to fulfillment (as reported in a 2005 *American Psychologist* article by M. E. P. Seligman, et al.) are kindness, fairness, authenticity, gratitude, and open-mindedness. Emotional strengths such as zest, gratitude, hope, and love are also more strongly associated with life satisfaction than are intellectual strengths. The article also reported that "Happy people are healthier, more successful, and more socially engaged." In other words, people who are happy and filled with gratitude and love attract back to themselves health, success, and social camaraderie.

ANCIENT IDEAS IN NEW THOUGHT

The Law of Attraction is sometimes associated with New Age thinking, but it is not new. In fact, its principles are very, very old. Different cultures have embraced these ideas in different forms, giving them a variety of names. But the basic concept is always the same: getting rid of negativity and focusing on positive thoughts makes room for healing, empowering energy that can change both you and the world around you.

In India, the concept is embodied in the idea of kundalini, a kind of psychospiritual energy, the energy of the consciousness. Kundalini means "coiled snake," and when the power of that coiled energy is tapped, a person will have a kundalini awakening—new states of consciousness and awareness, and even transcendence of self. As kundalini moves through the body, the energy gets rid of repressed and useless emotional blocks and heals the unfinished business of a person's life. There's a very similar concept in the Law of Attraction, which says that purging negativity makes room for one's desires to manifest.

In Hindu scriptures, a similar energy force is known as prana, which means "breath." Prana is a vital, life-sustaining force. It is the energy that controls all the bodily functions. Controlling prana can increase the vitality of the practitioner, and linking the prana to the cosmic energy inherent in the breath is believed to enable a person to transform himself in profound ways. This energy can also effect changes in other people and things; in other words, a thought can attract change even outside oneself.

In traditional Chinese medicine, this energy takes the form of chi (sometimes written as *qi*)—a Chinese word that literally means "air" or "breath." Chi is the flow of life energy. Chinese medicine practitioners believe that blockages and imbalances in the flow of chi give rise to illness. Balanced chi brings about good health. So another principle in both ancient beliefs and the Law of Attraction is that energy can heal the body. But there's more to it than that, because when you balance chi, you also come to a sense of peace and serenity. And when this harmony is achieved, your desires can then be fulfilled. Again, echoes of the Law of Attraction.

Outside of the physical, emotional, and mental realms are the actions we take in the world. Karma is a concept found in the Hindu, Jain, Sikh, and Buddhist religions. The word means "action" or "performance"; the idea is that your words and actions create your karma, and the nature of your karma shapes your experiences. This is similar to the concept in the Law of Attraction that energy exists in objects and thoughts and that a person's desires can be fulfilled by the energy her thoughts bring forth.

These are all Eastern religious ideas, but Western religions, too, express ideas that are found in the Law of Attraction. In Exodus, Moses led the Israelites through the desert for forty years as they went from slavery to their promised land. This steadfast determination to reach a goal by remaining focused on your desires is also found in the Law of Attraction. Their faith and vision as a group of people manifested what is known today as Israel.

In both the Old and New Testaments, faith is presented as a force that makes things happen. One of the core principles of the Law of Attraction is the ability of belief to cause physical changes in the universe—not just that belief motivates us to act, but that belief itself can cause real changes in the world. Judaism and Christianity also recognize the power of faith to bring about positive change in the world.

At the turn of the twentieth century, the Law of Attraction took on a kind of scientific meaning. It was sometimes referred to as the "energy of attraction," meaning the forces that come together when matter is created or the forces that hold atoms together. Other thinkers and philosophers claimed that thought was another force acting on the universe, in much the same way that light, gravity, and other natural forces do.

The Law of Attraction also became part of the New Thought movement, which today is known as New Age thought. (Interestingly, most New Age ideas—including the Law of Attraction—are based on age-old ideas that were swept away as science became the dominant philosophy in Western society. As I've already said, New Age thought is just a revival of very old ways of thinking about things.) The New Thought tradition dates to the 1880s. Proponents of the New Thought movement believe in the power of positive thinking and that anything is possible as long as you stay focused on positive thoughts. Ralph Waldo Emerson and Walt Whitman are among the well-known American writers who embraced New Thought.

The New Thought movement branched out into many groups and philosophies. For example, in 1927 Ernest Holmes established what eventually became the United Church of Religious Science. Holmes believed in what he called the Science of Mind. Science of Mind is a philosophy that integrates spiritual truths with science and physics. According to Holmes, intentions and ideas flow through a field of consciousness, which actually affects and creates the world around us. He said the secret to living a successful life is to consciously choose positive and productive thoughts.

The Law of Attraction has also been embraced by nonreligious groups. In 1952 Norman Vincent Peale published the book *The Power of Positive Thinking*. In it, he said that anyone could attain their goals and all obstacles could be removed by thinking positively. The book ended up on the *New York Times* bestseller list for 186 weeks, and Peale became internationally famous.

In 1984, Louise Hay published *You Can Heal Your Life*, which also remained on the *New York Times* bestseller list for years. The book promoted the idea that positive thoughts are the gateway to healing the body. Hay now runs a publishing company that counts Deepak Chopra and Wayne Dyer among its authors. In 2006, the Law of Attraction journeyed from the metaphysical realm to our mainstream culture when the book and movie *The Secret* were released. That same year, Esther and Jerry Hicks's book, *The Law of Attraction: The Basics* of the Teachings of Abraham, became a New York Times bestseller. Workshops and seminars about the Law of Attraction sprouted up across the nation.

Deepak Chopra, a physician and a proponent of holistic medicine, has written more than fifty books about New Thought ideas. He calls the energetic force behind the Law of Attraction a "field of pure consciousness or pure potentiality." He writes that without our consciousness or thoughts, the universe would have no physical reality. By tapping into this energetic field, he believes we can create—literally, on the physical level—the lives we desire.

THE LAW OF SOBRIETY

The Law of Sobriety takes the principles of the Law of Attraction and puts them to work for a specific purpose—to help individuals recover from addiction and alcoholism. The Law of Sobriety states that by taking certain action steps and applying your conscious energy to these steps, a life of peace and serenity is possible. The goal of the Law of Sobriety is to take actions in your recovery that will not only bring you sobriety, but will also bring you a life that is purposeful and meaningful.

The first step in the Law of Sobriety is finding your purpose with intention—this is the base upon which everything else rests. The next steps are living a life that is true to your values; living a life of authenticity; learning to live in appreciation, forgiveness, and compassion; living a life of right action; living with awareness and mindfulness; and learning to let go of resistance and attachments. In the following chapters, I will talk about each of these steps in depth.

The Law of Sobriety

Find your purpose with intention.

Live a life that is true to your values.

Live a life of authenticity.

Learn to live in appreciation, forgiveness, and compassion.

Live a life of right action.

Live with awareness and mindfulness.

Learn to let go of resistance and attachments.

When you embrace the Law of Sobriety, you realize your thoughts and emotions *do* make a difference. If you put negative thoughts and emotions out into the universe, that same negative energy will come back to you. For instance, if you believe you can never stay sober, you are going to be putting out a very negative vibration, and your actions will tend to make it difficult for you to stay sober. If you believe you can stay sober one day at a time, you are putting out positive thoughts. Those positive thoughts will attract the positive energy you need to make it a reality.

Of course, you also have to understand what you need to do to stay sober one day at a time. Does this mean you stay away from triggers, such as bars or old friends who still drink or use? Does it mean you get out of relationships that are bringing you down? Does it mean you find a job that is meaningful to you? The answers are different for everyone.

When it comes to emotions, do you live in fear or faith? If you feel you are not capable of making better relationship choices, changing that unfulfilling job for a satisfying one, or finding new sober friends, then it's time to make some shifts in your personal energy so that you can achieve these things. Remember, the Law of Attraction says that your life moves in the direction of your thoughts and emotions. If you are new to sobriety, it may take a while to remove the underlying fears that are holding you down. You have been numbing these fears for a long time. It's okay to acknowledge what you are afraid of; you can know your fear and still take the necessary actions to move forward.

The term "contrary action" is often mentioned in twelve-step programs. Basically, some people just have a bad sense of direction, and if they follow their natural inclinations, they end up doing the opposite of what is right for them. Instead, they need to take the "contrary action"—do the opposite of what their instincts tell them. The Law of Sobriety says that if you do what you are afraid to do because you know it's good for you, positive results will follow.

In truth, counterproductive thoughts that take you in the wrong direction are part of how you have been socialized. You were trained to believe them a very long time ago by your parents, your teachers, other people in your life, and even your environment. You heard these dysfunctional ideas so often that you internalized them and adopted them as your own. If you were acknowledged, praised, and brought up in a nurturing environment, perhaps your beliefs would have been different.

However, this is not to say that alcoholics and addicts only come from dysfunctional families, or that counterproductive thinking is somehow an "excuse" for substance abuse. There are many individuals who have struggled with mental illness, such as anxiety and depression, and have abused drugs and alcohol to self-medicate. Some alcoholics and addicts have a genetic predisposition for addiction and may have grown up in families with generations of alcoholism or addiction to other substances. And there are also people who have grown up in dysfunctional families who have never turned to drugs or alcohol. Each person's situation is unique.

None of us can change the past. But you have the opportunity right now to use the Law of Sobriety to make decisions that are healthy and that will put you in alignment with your true desires. It may also mean that now is the time to let go of those unhealthy people who are blocking the flow of your positive energy. Maybe your fear of losing someone or something is causing you to miss out on a more satisfying and fulfilling life or relationship. Fear is a powerful force, but if you stay in a situation that cannot possibly make you happy, then you have shut happiness out of your life.

Toxic Relationships

I can't tell you how many clients I've seen who are in verbally and sometimes physically abusive relationships. They want to be happy and rid themselves of depression and anxiety, and yet they cannot leave those relationships. Often their using and drinking are partly a result of the toxic energy-zappers they live with. Their resistance or fear stops them from moving forward—and then they wonder why they are still using or drinking.

If you are in an abusive relationship, it is literally sucking the life out of you. There is very little energy left for anything positive when you surround yourself with such a negative environment. The Law of Sobriety cannot work if you can't take the first steps to get out of the negative energy field you're living in. The only way to move forward is to shift the energy from negative to positive, from resistance to willingness to make changes—even if you are afraid of those changes.

If you're in an unhealthy relationship, maybe you're afraid you will be alone forever. Maybe you're afraid that you can't make it on your own financially, or maybe you don't believe you deserve anything or anyone better. These are just thoughts and emotions. Forgive yourself for having them and take the leap anyway—leave the relationship and believe you can have something better. The courage to move forward with the help of a professional, such as a psychotherapist, life coach, spiritual adviser, support group, or confidante, can help you take that next step.

Another idea that appears in twelve-step programs is to "detach with love." That means detaching yourself from a person's problems and behavior without feeling you must stop loving that person. Sometimes it is in your best interest to just stand back and observe a situation without trying to control it. You can't control other people, their actions, or their beliefs. You can only control your own reactions and the actions you decide to take. Instead of trying to control everything, maybe it's time to trust the universe to deal with the details of your life.

PUTTING THE LAW OF SOBRIETY TO WORK

In many ways, addicts and alcoholics are looking for a transcendent or mystical experience that will take them out of their misery and despair. When they use drugs or drink alcohol, they are hoping to be transported out of the intolerable reality in which they are living. Alcohol and drugs may provide addicts with a temporary escape, but eventually these substances turn on the addict and alcoholic and no longer relieve them of the pain and emptiness they feel every day.

Thinking about other people's stories can sometimes help us

understand things that have happened in our own lives. That's why, throughout this book, I'll tell you about some of the clients I've had who have struggled with issues you may also be facing. Of course, their names and other details about them have been changed. But the problems they faced and the solutions they found are very real.

Gary's Story

Gary was a client I had been seeing for several years who relapsed over the guilt and shame he felt after his addiction brought about the end of a five-year relationship. He'd had many years of sobriety, but he started drinking again. His drinking led to a progression of his alcoholism, and then he became hooked on crack cocaine. He started cheating on his longtime girlfriend with what he referred to as his "party girl." His girlfriend found out, they broke up, and his addiction eventually led to Gary losing his home and living under a freeway overpass.

Every time he tried to get sober, the memories of the pain he had caused his ex-girlfriend became so excruciating that he would use just to erase them. It became a cycle of brief sobriety, overwhelming guilt, then using to numb the pain, until trying to get sober was no longer possible for him. It wasn't until he reached the depth of his despair and became homeless that he was able to find sobriety again. The consequences of using became so great that he was willing to walk through his pain by getting sober, and work through all the feelings he had been trying to numb away with alcohol and drugs.

Addicts are on a spiritual quest of sorts, using mind-altering substances to move beyond their everyday existence. The difference between the spiritual quest of an addict and one of a mystic is that the mystic is seeking enlightenment and serenity and the addict is seeking nothingness. The addict's very core is empty; there's a soul sickness that some have described as a bottomless pit.

Regardless of what you call it, the addict and alcoholic are missing out on joy and will go to great lengths to search for it and escape their reality. Some people look at addicts and say that if they only put the same energy into their sobriety that they put into obtaining their drug of choice, their recovery would be assured. Of course, it's not that simple. But I do believe that if a person will allow the Law of Sobriety to work in his life—and take the action steps that go with it—that effort will be rewarded with a life of clarity and purpose. I have seen this over and over again with the clients I have had the privilege to work with. The action steps of the Law of Sobriety will enable you to clarify your life's purpose. They involve setting goals; following through and being accountable to those goals; living a life of authenticity that is true to your values; learning to live in appreciation, forgiveness, and compassion; and taking right action.

Affirmations

Affirmations are statements that describe what you want to happen in your life that you repeat over and over. They should be repeated with attention, conviction, and desire. You repeat them so that you can train your mind to stop bombarding you with negative thoughts. Many people spend a lot of time repeating negative words and statements in their minds: "I'll never get that job; that guy will never call; she didn't like me; I can't finish this; I'm lazy; I can't lose weight," and so on. Often, people repeat these negative statements without even being aware of it. But your subconscious mind accepts what you keep saying as the truth.

If you can teach your mind to repeat positive statements

Affirmations *(cont'd from page 23)*

rather than negative ones, your subconscious mind will accept the positive ideas as the truth. The repeated words help you focus on your aims and build positive mental images in your conscious mind; these positive images then affect the subconscious mind. The conscious mind—the mind you think with—starts the process, and then the subconscious mind takes over. And when that happens, your mind will be triggered into positive action. In fact, a 2006 article in *American Psychologist* (by M. E. P. Seligman, et al.) reported that interventions designed to help people identify and appreciate their own strengths and focus on the good things in their lives can decrease depression and make people lastingly happier.

By using this process consciously and sincerely, you can change your subconscious mind and transform your habits, behavior, attitude, and reactions—even reshape your life. For example, imagine that you get into arguments easily. You see this sometimes makes people uncomfortable, but you tell yourself, "That's just who I am. I have a bad temper. I can't let anything go." If you say that, you'll spend your life getting into arguments. Your mind forms a picture of you as a bad-tempered person and you act accordingly.

But if you say to yourself over and over with conviction, "I am an easygoing person. I know how to let the little things go," your mind forms a very different picture of you. And then you start to see yourself as a different person. You keep thinking and believing in yourself and soon you're having conversations where you disagree politely and then change the subject.

It's important to understand that repeating affirmations for a few minutes and then thinking negatively the rest of the day is not going to help you change. You have to push away the negative thoughts and train your mind to repeat positive ones instead.

The best affirmations are short and easy to remember. You should set aside some special time for yourself each day, maybe five or ten minutes, when you can concentrate on your affirmations and repeat them with clarity and purpose. You can also repeat them anytime your mind is not otherwise engaged—those times when negative thoughts tend to creep in—such as when you're waiting in line, riding the bus, or folding the laundry.

Frame your affirmation as a positive statement that is already happening now. So, for example, don't say "I will eventually learn to control my temper"; say "My temper is under control."

Here are some affirmations you might find useful in your life.

✓ I respect myself and I deserve recovery.
✓ I am learning to cope with my disease.
✓ I am learning to think first and not react to my emotions by drinking or using.
✓ I am learning to let go of fear and anxiety.
✓ I am learning to use the Law of Sobriety as a way to choose what thoughts I think.
✓ I am learning to handle situations that used to perplex me, without using or drinking.
✓ Walking through recovery helps me develop qualities of gratitude and forgiveness.
✓ I can have sober fun and accept all the healthy and appropriate pleasures of life.
✓ I can breathe, slow down, and let things go without acting impulsively.

The Law of Sobriety asks you to align yourself with your true purpose and take the necessary steps to get there. This enables you to access a deeper form of satisfaction with life. This source of unlimited joy is not available when you are a victim of your own self-destructive thoughts and behavior. When you connect instead to a universal life force, you have the capacity to create a life that is filled with harmony and peace. This is the serenity addicts and alcoholics are desperately seeking—but are looking for in all the wrong places.

The answers are inside of us, where they have been all along. We just didn't know how to access them because drugs or alcohol got in the way. How can a person access their inner essence when they are numbing themselves with chemicals? You cannot find your purpose if you are self-medicating. So first and foremost, you must be free of drugs and alcohol to begin your quest. Remember the movie *The Wizard of Oz*? The ruby slippers Dorothy was wearing always had the power to take her home. But she didn't know how to access their power until she learned some important lessons about what she could accomplish and what was really important to her.

Helen's Story

Helen was an only child. Her mother was an alcoholic who worked all day and then came home and drank until she passed out. She had very little time or energy for her daughter. Helen grew up feeling invisible, and she used men and alcohol to make herself seen and heard. She ended up in a marriage where alcohol and cocaine were always around. She had her own children, and while she was a better mother than her own mother had been, her alcoholism progressed and she could not stop drinking.

Then one night her daughter was having some friends sleep over and found Helen passed out in her bedroom. Her daughter was humiliated, and Helen realized that if she couldn't get sober for herself, she had to do it for her daughter. She needed to be the mother she always wanted to be—one who was different from her own mother. She managed to stop drinking on her own. But soon after, she lost her job due to the poor economy and began to have uncontrollable panic attacks. She could not go to the market, take her kids to school, or walk the dog without an overwhelming rush of terror that ripped through her entire body. She started seeing me for the panic attacks.

In the course of therapy, Helen realized she was having these attacks because the alcohol was no longer there to numb her. The rush of feelings she could no longer ignore were crippling her. All of the repressed emotions of her childhood bubbled up into her consciousness and had nowhere to go. The crises in her life brought into sharp focus all the years of trauma she had experienced as a child.

She began using the tools in the Law of Sobriety, along with attending Alcoholics Anonymous meetings, and the panic attacks subsided. She started to meditate; she began to do all of her activities mindfully—with her full attention—even if she was just washing dishes or doing the laundry. Each precious moment in her life was experienced fully, with her mind wide open instead of ruminating on thoughts of the past or fears for the future.

Helen also became aware of her codependency issues—her tendency to have relationships that were one-sided and emotionally destructive. She realized that by focusing exclusively on others and by keeping extraordinarily busy so that she wouldn't feel anything, she was losing herself and could not live an authentic life. It was time to grab hold of living by "being" rather than just existing by "doing."

She also realized that not having a two-parent family as a model when she was growing up meant she did not even know what a healthy relationship looked like. Helen is still in her dysfunctional marriage, but she realizes that to truly be who she is meant to be, she

will eventually have to leave her husband. Her overwhelming financial fears have immobilized her for now. And the trauma of growing
up in a single-parent family and not wanting to do that to her child
has left her frozen in old wounds.

As Helen continues to work through her fears, she gets closer and
closer to making choices that align with who she truly is. In her deepest being, she knows that living with an alcoholic who is not willing
to get sober is not in her or her daughter's best interests. Sometimes,
staying sober has to be enough until you are ready to take the leap
and trust the principles of the Law of Sobriety by embracing a life
that is truly living, rather than a life that is just surviving.

Throughout Helen's recovery process, she has had moments of
piercing clarity. She is learning that it is okay to live in the "unknown"—that is, the answers to life's biggest questions don't always
appear exactly when we need or want them. Sometimes we find these
gems of wisdom when we least expect them. There is no need to rush
our decisions. It is okay to take our time, slow down, and let the universe speak when it is ready. This understanding has helped release
some of the anxiety that had been building up inside Helen, so that
she can once again function in the ways she used to function. She is
able to go out and do things again. But she also has a whole new sense
of what is most important in her life. Worrying about finding a job
has been replaced with gratitude that she now can spend more time
with her children. She realizes that there might be another career
awaiting her but that for now staying home is "good enough." She
already has a plan for leaving her husband when she is ready, so it's
not necessary to live in anguish over the situation.

What's most important, for Helen and for anyone caught up in
addiction, is to believe in the Law of Sobriety, and that your truth will
reveal itself not because you are attached to finding the answer, but
rather through a quiet, still detachment that leaves space for the an-

swers to flow freely and effortlessly. Learning to celebrate your humanity and knowing that it is okay to have fun, love, laugh, and play is what truly living the Law of Sobriety is all about.

Whoever is happy will make others happy too. He who has courage and faith will never perish in misery.

—From *The Diary of Anne Frank*

THE POWER OF FELLOWSHIP

It's important to mention here that the Law of Sobriety worked in Helen's life in conjunction with the twelve-step meetings she attended. At meetings, she became part of a group of like-minded individuals who were all there for the purpose of staying sober. The power of the group and their collective consciousness is so strong that I believe this is often what keeps alcoholics and addicts sober; this was certainly true for Helen.

As I said in the introduction, the Law of Sobriety will work for you even if you decide you cannot attend a twelve-step program. If you work on each part of the Law of Sobriety with clarity and focus, you will be able to change your life. But being part of a group makes the process easier for many people. Alcoholics Anonymous groups are also called fellowships, and they work together with a common purpose and goal. Their purpose and intention is so strong that the group as a whole attracts back to themselves their intention to stay sober—thus enabling the Law of Sobriety to do its work.

Tools for Change
Finding the Meaning in Your Life

There are several tools I have used to help myself and my clients reach their desired state. These include meditation, intention statements, visualizations, questions to ask yourself, and affirmations. Throughout the book, I will give you suggestions for how to use these tools to work on the specific step in the chapter.

These tools enable you to have a concrete way to embrace the Law of Sobriety with clarity and focus. Meditation can give you the harmony, balance, and peace to begin your day. Intentions provide you with a method to keep track of your daily goals. Asking yourself, the universe, or your higher power questions helps bring forth your inner wisdom and intuition. Daily visualizations provide you with the opportunity to envision a multitude of infinite possibilities that await you. And affirmations can be a powerful way to energize positive thoughts of yourself, your desires, and your sobriety.

We'll start with some questions. The Law of Sobriety says that if you have meaning in your life and are using your energy for what you are meant to be doing on this planet, it is only natural that you will succeed. So ask yourself:

- Am I in a healthy relationship?
- Am I doing work that I am committed to?
- Am I accessing a spiritual life that sustains me?
- Am I grateful for the little things?
- Do I live as an authentic human being or continue to live as my false self?
- Do I take steps that match my values?
- Am I aware and mindful of each precious moment?
- Am I willing to let go of the results and enjoy the process of living?

Ask the universe or your innermost being these questions while breathing in, then slowly breathe out. Allow these questions to inspire you and guide you to the answers that have always been inside of you. Don't concern yourself if the answers don't come right away. Your answers are waiting to be discovered at just the right time and not a moment sooner, so relax and enjoy the process. The unknown is only temporary.

TWO

Finding Your Purpose
with Intention

You can be anything you want to be,
do anything you set out to accomplish,
if you hold to that desire with singleness of purpose.

—Abraham Lincoln

The Law of Sobriety is about living your life on purpose, clean and sober, and mustering up all the energy you have to go after exactly what you want. You are not only going after sobriety, but are also pursuing whatever it is that brings you joy. Discovering your life purpose in sobriety may be the most important breakthrough you will ever make; it may even save your life. Deciding why you are here and what gives your life meaning keeps you on track by enabling you to choose where to put your energy.

Every person provides the energy—good or bad—that powers his or her own life. You create the energy that moves through you so you can achieve and maintain your sobriety. The Law of Sobriety itself is a compelling illustration of how, by focusing your energy on your sobriety, you have the power to enact your own recovery and even determine how satisfying it will be. But life should be about more than just survival. You are here to use your energy to attain what really matters most to you. The idea of this first step is to become a *conscious* source of energy—to direct your energy where you want it to go.

Living on purpose and with intention means living with focus and clarity, with self-determination and an insatiable appetite to be the best you can be. It's about getting out of a negative mind-set, turning up the positive frequency, and going after what you most desire—starting with sobriety.

WHAT IS PURPOSE?

What exactly is *purpose*? One of my favorite definitions comes from *Becoming a Professional Life Coach* by Patrick Williams and Diane S. Menendez: "[Purpose is] our compelling reason for living. It gives meaning to our work and our life. It guides our choices. Some people describe their purpose as their 'calling.' Whatever we call it, it profoundly shapes the direction of our life." Just enduring life without passion, meaning, and purpose will keep you stuck in the same old patterns that led you to addiction. It can also be a contributing factor in developing depression, anxiety, physical illnesses, and mental health issues. So often, my clients will come to my office believing they have some type of mental illness, such as depression, and in fact, some do. However, some of them simply lack direction or motivation. When you have no purpose, you may feel justified to use drugs or alcohol and not get clean and sober. In fact, I believe that without purpose and passion, some type of relapse is inevitable. Perhaps you won't drink or use, but you will definitely have a hard time maintaining your emotional sobriety—the emotional balance and stability that makes it possible to be happy and productive and feel more alive.

When you truly believe that your life is filled with purpose and you have precious gifts to offer, you will be strongly motivated to work your chosen recovery program and experience the full benefits of sobriety.

—From *The Wellness-Recovery Connection* by John Newport, Ph.D.

Going through a twelve-step program, attending meetings, getting a sponsor, seeing a psychotherapist, and doing everything else you can to stay sober is likely not enough if there isn't something beyond sobriety that drives and motivates you. There are so many spiritual and physical options today that offer a way to maintain a sense of balance and well-being. You can take up meditation, prayer, yoga, tai chi, acupuncture, energy healing, crystal healing, chakra healing, Reiki, biofeedback, neurofeedback—they all have their place. However, it is the power of purpose that will make the difference in your ability to live a life that aligns with your dreams and desires.

Meditation

Often alcoholics and addicts are impulse-driven by their immediate need for gratification. Their inability to cope with stress, frustration, disappointment, anger, fear, and resentment keeps them in old, self-defeating patterns that include drinking and using drugs. In fact, they are following unconscious patterns that are familiar and therefore require less effort. Without a conscious awareness of these thoughts and behaviors and an intention to change direction, they fall into the same self-damaging patterns over and over again.

Meditation is one of the tools you can use to get out of this rut. By learning to just be still and breathe, you are able to take a step away from yourself and look at your life from the outside. This objectivity will help you begin to deal with issues head-on and with courage.

Meditation offers other benefits as well. Physical changes in the body have been documented during meditation, including altered metabolism, heart rate, respiration, blood pressure, and brain chemistry. Meditation has also been associated with a stronger immune response and faster healing times. Studies have found meditation enables people to better cope with pain and stress, as well. Relaxation, better concentration, a different state of awareness, a rest from the incessant activity of the mind, and being able to maintain a self-observing attitude are some of the behavioral benefits.

Alcoholics and addicts tend to be driven by their impulses. One consequence of this is transient thinking, which means they do not reason things through. Instead, they simply respond to whatever is going on around them according to how they feel at the moment. Meditation enables a person to take a pause and get out of that cycle of simply acting on impulse. As a friend of mine in a twelve-step program says, meditation helps a person "make the journey from his mind to his heart." It offers a temporary reprieve from the mental chatter and demands that are constantly taking up our attention.

Silencing the inner voice is not easy at first. After all, it's been chattering away in your head all your life! Thoughts will keep creeping in. Just watch them go by with no judgment, as if they were runaway balloons floating in the sky. Experienced meditators call this phase "monkey mind," because your mind keeps jumping around and chattering away. Don't think you have somehow failed because your mind is jumping around. *Everyone* starts out with monkey mind.

Meditation is one of those things you get better at the more you do it. Just sitting down and doing it, no matter what the immediate result, improves your meditation practice. As you learn to quiet your mind, the process of meditation takes on its own energy. In that quiet space where your judgmental, impatient, demanding inner voice no longer speaks, your mind will be clear and clean. And in that place you will find peace and refreshment—what you have been seeking but never finding through drugs and alcohol. The Law of Sobriety says answers will come to you that have been drowned out for too long by that chattering inner voice. Your true self can finally be heard. The stillness of meditation, although it will not replace your cravings, does make space for your innate wisdom to come forth, so that personal fulfillment is at last possible.

PURPOSE PREVENTS RELAPSE

You may have heard that addicts and alcoholics concentrate on staying sober one day at a time or even one minute at a time, and that's all they can accomplish. This is true in the beginning stages of recovery, and for some people it remains true for years into their clean and sober lives. However, unless you are fulfilled by something more, you run a big risk of getting stuck in the vortex of misery that made you use or drink in the first place. When you have no purpose, you may feel justified to use again and not stay clean and sober.

Alex's Story

Alex spent his days at work and his nights locked up in his study at home, snorting cocaine. His family didn't know he had a problem. He was the CEO of a very large company and was afraid someone would find out about his addiction to cocaine. Even though all twelve-step programs promise to maintain the anonymity of those who attend, he refused to go for fear of being found out.

I had been seeing Alex on and off for about a year. We had been making progress, and Alex was no longer using. But when the economy took a turn for the worse and his company began to have major financial problems, he suddenly found himself under enormous stress to not only keep his business open, but to find a way to pay his employees. The fact that his whole identity had been built around his company only compounded Alex's stress. This pressure was a sure setup for a relapse. He became overwhelmed with despair and hopelessness. His inability to hold things together was pulling him back to a dark place. His need to numb himself began to feel irresistible.

I did some life coaching with Alex to help him discover what he wanted out of the different areas of his life. I gave him an exercise tool known as the Wheel of Life to help him figure out how much time he was devoting to different areas of his life. The life sections of the wheel included physical environment, career, money, health, fun and recreation, personal growth, and family and friends. When Alex worked with the Wheel of Life, he discovered an enormous imbalance. His personal growth and time with family and friends needed an energy surge. He had so isolated himself by spending every evening alone using cocaine that he'd neglected his wife and children. (You can see an example of the Wheel of Life and get an idea of how it works at http://www.mindtools.com/pages/article/newHTE_93.htm.)

Our work together involved helping him to see the value of having a more intimate relationship with his wife and spending more quality time with his family. When he began to feel more balance in his personal life, he spent less time locked up in his study and more time enjoying activities with his family. He started to go to church on Sundays, started coaching his son's Little League team, and created a "date night" for himself and his wife. Once he broke out of his isolation and began devoting his energy to his family, his relapses ended. He was no longer living in his head night after night, alone with his thoughts of inadequacy and worthlessness because his company was struggling. The Law of Sobriety gave him a second chance in life by bringing a sense of purpose and meaning to a life that had been right there waiting for him the whole time.

When you have a sense of your own identity and vision of where you want to go in your life, you then have the basis for reaching out to the world and going after your dreams for a better life.
—From *You Can Make It Happen Every Day*
by Stedman Graham

Relapse can also result from going through a sobriety program without purpose and passion. I have heard people say in twelve-step meetings that "the novelty has worn off" or "I am no longer looking at my sobriety through rose-colored glasses." What they are really saying is, "I have no purpose in my life. Beyond getting sober, I don't know what I really, really want out of life." In fact, most people never actually ask themselves what they really, really want. Most of us become socially conditioned to believe we should do this or be that, and we just fall into patterns without thinking much about them. And some of us lack the courage to try to break out of the patterns we have fallen into.

FEAR HOLDS US BACK

One of the biggest reasons you keep yourself from moving forward and finding your purpose is fear—fear of rejection, the unknown, failure, or even fear of success. When you live in fear, you are sure to be putting out negativity into the universe. How can anything positive come out of constantly living in fear? Your self-sabotaging thoughts will return to you exactly the pessimism you are vibrating.

One of the hallmarks of addiction and alcoholism is fear of what the future will bring. Often this fear is rooted in things that have happened in the past that you hold on to and continue to worry about. And often fear of the future is not based in reality. In twelve-step programs, fear is known as an acronym for FALSE EVIDENCE APPEARING REAL. In other words, you worry about problems that don't even exist. There is no possibility of living a purposeful life if you are not living in the present, where you can take action, achieve your goals, and fulfill your dreams.

Suzanne's Story

Suzanne was trying to become an actress. She had all the training one could possibly have for this career. She had a high-powered agent, a supportive husband, and all the connections she needed to land a part in either television or film. Suzanne came to see me because she was constantly doubting herself. Every time she left a casting call, she would immediately dive into a negative tailspin. She compared herself unfavorably to the other actresses auditioning for the part, berated herself for not already being a success, and was convinced that she had failed the audition. Then she'd go home and drink away her self-loathing and self-doubt. Suzanne could not let go of the negative chatter in her head—her fear of failure and her conviction that her negative thoughts represented reality.

By embracing so much negativity, Suzanne was slowly turning her fears into reality. I taught her how to reframe these negative thoughts to create more uplifting and optimistic ones. Instead of embracing failure after an audition, she needed to affirm success, even if she didn't believe it. I asked her to tell herself that she was one of the best actresses for the part. When she began to imagine other actresses getting the part, I asked her to picture herself playing the role instead. I encouraged her to embody the role of a successful actress with every part of her being. When she thought about not already being a famous actress, I asked her to picture herself at an awards ceremony, walking up to the podium and accepting an award for her outstanding acting.

Although these exercises seemed silly to her at first, they gave her something to focus on other than her fears. They also enabled Suzanne to be more relaxed and confident when she went on auditions, because she was able to stop listening to the negative, fearful voices in her head and be in the present. She realized her fears had been keeping her from being in the moment when she auditioned for parts. By being fully present and putting out positive energy, she embraced her career in a whole new way. Embodying the Law of Sobriety enabled her to focus her energy on believing in herself wholeheartedly, rather than living in fear of failure and doubt about her abilities.

Tools for Change
What Do You Desire?

Let's play pretend. Imagine you are a child again, without worries or anxieties. Remember those feelings you had of wonder and curiosity? Just let go and remember what that felt like. Go back and reexperience the joy and excitement you felt. Let them resonate all through your body. Feel the energy flow from that deep place in your soul. Think about everything you wanted to have, to do, to be. Embody with all your senses—sight, sound, taste, smell, touch—what it would feel like to be what you dreamed of becoming. Did you want to be an actress? Did you want to be a doctor? Did you want to build houses? Did you want to be a pilot?

Now come forward a few years. What stopped you from pursuing those dreams? Were you told that what you wanted to do would not make a practical career? Were you told there wasn't enough money to go to college? Were you told your dreams were just crazy ideas? Were you told very few people make it in your dream career? Did you believe you were not good enough or capable of achieving such a dream?

We all have been that little child with dreams of the future, but somewhere along the way those happy, hopeful images were replaced with fears, anxieties, doubts, and the belief that they could never happen. Did you feel undeserving? It's time to access the positive energy of the universe to make your dreams a reality.

What is it going to take to fulfill your deepest desires? What is your next step going to be? What would you want if anything was possible? The answers will come, as long as you tap into the Law of Sobriety. Don't worry about how long it's going to take to get there or whether your dreams will be fulfilled exactly the way you want them to be. In twelve-step programs we say, "Don't quit until the miracle happens." Trust that opportunities await you, as long as you stay focused on what you desire.

ADDING INTENTION

We've talked a lot about purpose. Now let's define *intention*. When you profoundly desire something and make it your objective to obtain the object of your desire, you have intention. So finding your purpose with intention means figuring out what motivates you and makes living meaningful, then taking action to make that happen.

Finding your purpose with intention is not necessarily about sitting down and making a specific plan for how you are going to get there. The how will come later, when you have clarity about what is calling you to action. When you focus only on the how, your options for reaching your goals seem to shrink. For example, if your goal is sobriety, there are many options for achieving it, including twelve-step programs, rehab facilities, outpatient programs, psychotherapy, integrative medicine, life coaching, recovery coaching, religious or spiritual avenues, and a host of other options. Asking *what you want* allows you to discover the many paths that will get you there. Focusing on *how to do it* can keep you stuck in the same old solutions that may not have worked for you. The more choices you have, the better chance you have of picking one that is right for you—and of fulfilling your purpose and no one else's.

So intention is about having the resolve to get where you want to go. It's not about following one specific path, but about being open to taking whatever path will get you there. You intend—with all your energy—to achieve your purpose. When you are questioning your sobriety, you know—because you have the intention and the resolve—that while it may sometimes feel like an uphill journey, it can be an enjoyable one, because you know your destination, and you know the struggle will get you the reward you seek. When you have a purpose with intention, even those difficult steps lead you to where you want to go.

Sometimes the journey takes a left turn, and you suddenly find yourself with a new purpose. You realize that when you give yourself the room to move forward, anything and everything is possible. For example, perhaps you decide to go on a diet to lose weight. Then you read in a magazine that your diet would be more effective if you also exercise, so you start walking thirty minutes a day and lifting small weights three times a week. You begin to not only feel stronger, but your body tone and flexibility are improving, too. Now your original purpose with intention has morphed into not only losing weight but exercising as well. In this particular case, although losing weight can be slow and frustrating, the fact that there is now an added benefit of feeling powerful through exercise makes the journey not only tolerable, but also enjoyable.

Having a purpose with intention can motivate you and give you the will to stop drinking and using right now. If you focus your energy on what you want, the Law of Sobriety says that what you focus on will happen. By focusing on the ultimate goal of sobriety and, beyond that, a life of meaning and purpose, your behaviors will naturally follow this desire. You will know the Law of Sobriety is at work in your life.

Lack of Purpose and Substance Abuse

Researchers at UCLA found a link between lack of purpose, substance abuse, and suicidal thoughts in adolescents. The 2006 study by Lisa L. Harlow, et. al., began by hypothesizing that depression and low self-worth may lead to a lack of purpose in life, which in turn may lead to suicidal thoughts and substance abuse. But the researchers found some important differences in cause and effect, and in outcome, based on sex. Young men with feelings of depression and low self-worth were more likely to turn to drugs and alcohol, while young women were more likely to consider suicide. Young men who felt they lacked a purpose in life were more likely to think of suicide. Young women without purpose turned to substance abuse.

Tools for Change
Uncovering Your Purpose

One way to help organize your thoughts about your life purpose is by asking yourself some questions and writing down the answers. The process of organizing and writing down your thoughts can help clarify your current situation and how you would like to move forward in your recovery. Keeping track of your progress will also remind you of how much you have accomplished.

1. On a sticky notepad, a journal, or a lined piece of paper, make a list of five things you would like to accomplish that will enrich your recovery process. Do this by completing the sentence, "My recovery is enriched when_____." (Examples might be, "My recovery is enriched when I attend twelve-step meetings five days a week" or "My recovery is enriched when I meditate for twenty minutes a day.")

2. Ask yourself what you are tolerating in your life that keeps you from accomplishing your recovery goals or life purpose goals. Complete the sentence, "I cannot reach my recovery goals because_____." (Examples might be, "I cannot reach my recovery goals because I continue to resist meeting with my sponsor" or "I cannot reach my recovery goals because my attention is on others rather than on myself.")

3. List five action steps you will take in the coming week to begin reaching your recovery and life purpose goals, so you can fulfill your deepest desires. (Examples might be making a structured daily schedule that includes attending twelve-step meetings, calling your sponsor, meditating for at least ten minutes a day, and reminding yourself just before you go to bed of what you are grateful for. Or you might make a list of triggers that could cause you to relapse and write down what you will do to avoid those triggers. If you are stuck about what some of your life purpose goals are, your action steps might include

participating in new activities that make you feel confident or strengthen a positive image you have of yourself.)

4. At the end of the week, ask yourself, "What have I done this week toward reaching my recovery goals?" (Examples might be, "I attended three meetings this week" or "I became more aware this week of what triggers me to use.")

5. Now that you know what you have accomplished this week, complete the sentence, "I feel_____as I move closer to reaching my purpose." (Examples might be, "I feel proud I was able to accomplish the goals I set out for myself this week" or "I feel empowered and recharged after going to a twelve-step meeting.")

Thinking About Yourself in a New Way

The Law of Sobriety demands that you take personal responsibility for the thoughts you put out into the universe. Your thoughts are where your deep convictions lie, where intention lives and breathes, and where your life force is expressed.

One of the first steps is to stop thinking of yourself as an addict or alcoholic. I know this goes against the principles of twelve-step programs, but I do believe that by continuing to label yourself that way, you drag around the baggage that goes with the label. Quite simply, the Law of Sobriety says that what you call yourself, you will become. So often I see clients who are chronic relapsers, and when they continue to identify themselves as an addict or an alcoholic, it seems to give them the permission to relapse: "I'm an alcoholic so I drink" or "I use because I'm an addict."

I'm not making any judgments about relapses. I know relapse is part of the disease of addiction, and slipping back into disease is always a possibility if you've had a drug or alcohol addiction. However, labeling yourself in a negative way can sabotage your efforts to stay sober.

I believe calling yourself a *recovering* alcoholic or a *recovering* addict is more useful—and more accurate—because that is what you are becoming and is precisely what you want to continue to manifest. This is a positive and optimistic way to address yourself. It's also a way to give yourself the credit you deserve for all the work you are putting into your sobriety. In fact, don't even think of it as work. Following the Law of Sobriety is not work; you are becoming the person you are meant to be right now, in this very moment.

LETTING GO OF FAULTY JUDGMENTS

Another step to living your life on purpose and with intention is letting go of faulty judgments—incorrect conclusions about yourself—that no longer serve you and never did. These negative belief systems are blocking you from moving forward toward your goals. Examples of faulty judgments include feelings of inadequacy or worthlessness. Perhaps you had a boss who treated you unfairly or a past lover who broke up with you without any valid reason. Yes, those experiences are painful. But they often say more about the other person than they do about you. If you continue to hold on to the beliefs you attach to these negative experiences, you are only going to create more negativity in your life.

You are much more than the roles you play in your life. The Law of Sobriety says that your self-esteem is directly related to how you see yourself and whether or not you believe you are a valuable person.

You have a soul and an essence that goes far beyond being a mother or father, a sister or brother, a friend or neighbor. The type of job you hold is only a label; it isn't the essence of who you are inside. Until you let go of these faulty judgments, a purposeful life will elude you.

No one can make you feel inferior without your consent.

—From *This Is My Story*
by Eleanor Roosevelt

Sometimes these faulty judgments about yourself are a result of a childhood trauma that has not been resolved. For example, if you were neglected as a baby or toddler and there was no one to give you the love, nurturing, and acknowledgment you needed to grow up with a healthy sense of self, you most likely felt invisible. This could lead to believing that your thoughts, desires, opinions, and feelings don't matter, and that, as a person, you don't matter either. You become the person who falls between the cracks.

When I work at addiction treatment centers, often there are clients who try to remain unnoticed. They don't want to make waves or call any attention to themselves. They rarely speak up in groups or complain if they are unhappy about something. This behavior is very rare in a rehab facility; most clients who are getting off drugs and alcohol have something to say about everything. They no longer have their drugs of choice to keep them numb, so every feeling they experience comes right to the surface.

However, there is always that one client who seems likable, is easy to get along with, and always appears to be focused on others. That person is literally denying his or her own wants, needs, and feelings, and this makes the recovery process very difficult. My work is to help those clients see that they do matter and that they are not invisible. Their feelings of being nonexistent come from belief systems they internalized a very long time ago that were based on faulty judgments about themselves.

Perhaps these belief systems were used as defense mechanisms to deal with the helplessness and pain they felt in growing up in an abusive or neglectful home. It can take all of a child's energy just to gain some distance from the chaos and inconsistency of living in a dysfunctional family. There is no safety or nurturing in such an environment. Children from these homes often become "parentified"—they are expected to take care of their parents' needs and are therefore always focused on others. This leads to the neglect of their own wants and needs.

In this traumatic environment, children learn they cannot count on their parents, and they lose all faith and trust in everything, everyone, and, most important, in themselves. They take on their parents' problems and may even believe they are at fault because their parents drink, use drugs, are depressed, or even abuse them. They feel guilty and responsible for their own pain.

Their parents are not present, so they also feel invisible. They take on adult responsibilities that they can't possibly master, and so they are trapped in a situation where it is inevitable that they will fail. They begin to feel inadequate or think of themselves as failures. How can these feelings possibly allow for positive energy to flow into their lives?

When you're not aware of the faulty judgments you make about yourself, destructive behavior and patterns of thinking can develop. Your positive energy becomes blocked and this makes moving forward in your life impossible. Deeply ingrained fears and anxieties prevent your creative processes from awakening and you find yourself stuck, repeating the same old stories to yourself: "I'm not good enough," "I will never be able to stay sober," "I don't deserve anything better," "I will never find the right relationship."

It is time to tell yourself that the faulty judgments you held on to as a young child no longer work for you, just as using alcohol and drugs no longer work. You must believe that you are no longer that helpless child, but are instead an empowered adult living a life of purpose, meaning, and sobriety. Those old imprinted ideas can keep you in the cycle of addiction and alcoholism. When you remove those obstacles, transformation is possible; new opportunities present themselves and you can begin to fulfill your deepest desires.

If you continue to focus as you have been, to think as you have been, and to believe as you have been, then nothing in your experience will change.
—From *The Law of Attraction: The Basics of the Teachings of Abrahan*
by Esther and Jerry Hicks

Cindy's Story

Cindy grew up with parents who were both heroin addicts. When they divorced, she was constantly shuffled from household to household. Each of her parents had a barrage of different relationships, and strangers were always coming in and out of Cindy's life. She was molested by several of her mother's boyfriends, but was told by her mother to keep quiet about the abuse. Often, such predators were the only source of support for Cindy's mother, who feared that if her current boyfriend left, her drug supply would vanish and she and her daughter would be out on the street.

Her mother's addiction meant that from a very young age, Cindy was forced to live with uncertainty and without safety. When she became a teenager, Cindy started repeating her mother's pattern of forming relationships with abusive men. All of her energy was focused on these unhealthy relationships, and she had no energy left to figure out who she was, what she wanted, or what her purpose was. How could she? She was in survival mode. This pattern persisted into her twenties. Drugs and alcohol became Cindy's refuge to escape the unbearable pain she felt.

Cindy struggled with an addiction to pain medication for years. It wasn't until much later that she found a healthier relationship with a man who actively supported her recovery process. Once she finally experienced the safety and nurturing she never received growing up, she also felt strong enough to seek medical help through an outpatient psychiatrist, and was ultimately able to get clean and sober by ridding herself of her dependence on pain medications.

Dwell not on the past. Use it to illustrate a point, then leave it behind. Nothing really matters except what you do now in this instant of time. From this moment onwards you can be an entirely different person, filled with love and understanding, ready with an out-stretched hand, uplifted and positive in every thought and deed.

—From *Thinking from the Infinite*
by Carell Zaehn

But even though she had the life she dreamed of with someone who loved and adored her, Cindy constantly felt stuck. She found herself starting but never finishing projects, classes, and even jobs. She couldn't understand why she could not move forward in her life. Once she started attending weekly psychotherapy sessions, she was able to come to terms with the trauma she had suffered while growing up in a very sick family. She discovered she was still carrying the feelings of not being good enough that she felt as a child and teenager. She still held on to the childhood message she had internalized, that she could "never amount to anything." Deep in her core, she believed this was so. The Law of Sobriety says you attract the energy you resonate, and Cindy was attracting the negativity she had grown up internalizing.

Finally, Cindy made a conscious decision to disengage from her biological family. They appeared to be jealous and resentful of the life she now lived and expressed their bitterness and disapproval whenever she communicated with them. She needed to cut them off so she could move on with her life. Their negativity was toxic, and these poisonous conversations were triggers that could lead to relapse. Nothing in her life was worth relapsing over—especially having a relationship with parents who had no idea how to parent her.

For Cindy to let go of her faulty judgments, she first had to realize, consciously, that these beliefs were cemented in her psyche, and then understand how they got there. She had to learn to let them go and to embrace a new, reality-based understanding of herself and her potential. When she did this, she broke out of her cycle of immobilization and realized the many possibilities that were before her.

Cindy went back to school and became the person she always wanted to be. It was only by releasing her attachment to her past that she was able to create the space to succeed and follow her passions. The past cannot be changed, but you always have the opportunity to change the way you interpret and understand it.

If I am not for myself, who will be for me?

—Rabbi Hillel

THE ENERGY OF THE PEOPLE AROUND YOU

To live your life on purpose, you need to surround yourself with people who align with your purpose. If you spend your time with people who are still using, you are taking on their negative energy vibrations; instead of thinking about recovery and what your true purpose is, you begin behaving in ways that go against your intentions and goals. Clients of mine who want to get sober but hang out with their buddies who are still using find it is a complete mismatch and is self-defeating. You need to align yourself with people who are sober. You automatically change your negative energy when you remove yourself from the environments and people associated with using, and the path away from addiction opens up.

In her book *Spiritual Fitness,* Caroline Reynolds writes, "The first thing to remember is that many of your emotions do not even originate with you—you are picking them up from the people around you." In Cindy's case, she had to let go of the negative feelings she had learned from her parents. Only then was she able to replace them with positive ones she got from being in a healthy, loving, stable relationship. When you follow the Law of Sobriety, you take your cues from people who resonate health, love, and honesty.

In twelve-step programs, people are often advised to "act as if." For example, if you believe you can't stay sober because you just can't change, act as if you are already transforming. Seem simplistic? Absolutely, but it works. If you are feeling helpless and frustrated by your attempts at sobriety, act as if you believe you will be successful. If you just don't trust your feelings, act as if all of your feelings are okay and a natural extension of who you are. Maybe you are feeling a disconnect between your mind, body, and spirit. Just tell yourself, "My mind, body, and spirit are connected, and I am continuing to integrate them to experience peace and serenity," and then act as if you really are feeling peaceful and serene. Doing this can help you develop new ways of navigating the world—ways you may not have considered while growing up in a dysfunctional family.

Of course, if you've never acted as if you're sober, confident, or capable, it can be difficult to know what to do when you're acting "as if." The answer is to surround yourself with like-minded, positive, successful individuals. Model yourself after them, and the Law of Sobriety says the energy of your actions and theirs will bring those qualities into your life.

I think of my own mother as an example of learning how to act "as if" by emulating the behaviors and actions of others. My mother's parents were compulsive gamblers. While Sundays were family days in most of her friends' homes, my mother's parents hosted poker parties instead. It was all about gambling for my grandparents, and on those days my mother became invisible in her own home. Gambling was such an obsession with my grandmother that while she lay dying from cancer at a local hospital, her fourth husband stole everything out of her apartment. After my grandmother died, my mother had nothing to keep as a remembrance of the woman who gave birth to her.

Obviously, my mother did not have an ideal childhood. Her parents could not be family role models for her. When she got married and gave birth to me and my brother, she had no frame of reference for what being a good mother and creating a healthy family life was all about. And yet, she managed to do it. She told me she would watch how other mothers whom she regarded as "normal" navigated their family life. In this way, she learned about family traditions and typical family dinners, outings, and holidays. As a result, we always had dinners as a family, my mother always made sure we were dressed properly, we went on family vacations, and there were always parties for birthdays and holidays. These were things my mother never had as a child, but she managed, by modeling the behavior of others, to figure out how to give them to us. As a single mother, I wished I could have done half the things my mother did to keep our family together. She really did the very best she could, even though there were no role models for her to follow when she was growing up.

My mother is an example of how, when we really want something and are determined to go after it, the universe brings us exactly what we need. Is there something in your life that you would like to change but are not sure how to go about it? Maybe it's time to ask your higher power, or ask the universe, for what you need to make your sobriety possible and your recovery fulfilling. If you project the energy of self-assuredness and know the answers will come, the Law of Sobriety says they will.

Tools for Change
Finding Your Purpose With Intention

So how do you find your purpose with intention? You start not by asking questions, but by being quiet. It is in this stillness that you will find your purpose. You will begin to understand exactly what you want out of sobriety and how you are going to get there. Try these exercises to access your purpose with intention.

• Spend ten to twenty minutes a day focusing just on your breathing. Take full breaths right into your belly and notice what arises in your body during each moment. Notice with curiosity and a sense of wonder what the universe is trying to tell you. What is the wisdom in your body trying to impart to you? Notice how the recovering addict or alcoholic in you feels. Observe your recovering self and assess what that feels like. Greet that part of yourself with profound compassion and allow the truths about your life that you have long kept buried to unfold.

• Imagine yourself in a safe and nurturing environment and notice what arises as you visualize yourself in this peaceful and serene place. Notice what this stillness feels like in your body. Name this place and know that its innate wisdom is always there for you to access. There are no limits to what you will discover in this beautiful sanctuary, this place of innate knowing.

• Ask yourself the following questions by closing your eyes, breathing in the questions, and breathing out the answers.

✓ What do I want from my sobriety?

✓ What are my goals in recovery?

✓ Does my environment match my purpose?

✓ Do the people in my life align with who I am and who I am becoming?

✓ What am I willing to do to live with purpose?

✓ How, when, and where will I have the opportunity to express my purpose?

✓ Is my energy focused on the goal of sobriety?

You may need to ask yourself these questions more than once to really hear the answers. But don't second-guess yourself. If the answer you receive in your place of stillness seems unlikely to your "rational" mind, don't discard it. This may just be your old negative patterns and faulty judgments trying to hold you back. The point of this exercise is to let go and notice whatever comes up without having an agenda or looking for the specific answer to a specific question. Just switch off your inner repressive judgments and lovingly observe whatever pops out of your subconscious.

Once you have answered these questions, create purpose statements or affirmations about your life purpose. An affirmation provides you with the wisdom to know what your true purpose is right now and not what you hope it will be in the distant future. Write these statements down, so you can go back to them as a reminder and repeat them whenever you need them. For example, you might write:

✓ My purpose is to have a healthy lifestyle that excludes drinking and using.

✓ My purpose is to live in the present moment without fear, resentment, or anger.

✓ My intention is to live in harmony with the universe.

✓ My purpose is to be there for my family as a clean and sober person.

✓ My purpose is to align myself with people, places, and things that make me feel full of joy.

✓ My intention is to align my energy with what I have been put here to do on this planet.

✓ My intention is to listen to the universe and its infinite wisdom when in doubt.

These statements will be your guiding force in everything you say and do. They will give you clarity and intention in all of your actions with others and yourself. By following your purpose, you clear the way for your authentic self to emerge. Not only will you enjoy the richness of sobriety, but you will achieve whatever you focus your intention and energy on. You will achieve what you desire.

THREE

Living a Life That Is True to Your Values

---

*Blessed are they who translate every good thing
they know into action, for ever higher truths
shall be revealed unto them.*

—Peace Pilgrim

Most of the values you held as a child were learned from your parents, friends, teachers, and the society in which you lived. As you moved into adolescence, the values you had accepted in your youth no longer resonated with who you were becoming. As you attempted to gain your own identity, you may have rebelled against those early value systems. You may have started experimenting with drugs and alcohol due to peer pressure. You may have felt the need to self-medicate to cope with the growing pains of adolescence or with the pain of living in a dysfunctional family. You started to steer away from your core values because you were confused about what they were and the external world began to have a stronger influence on you. You began to lose sight of your true self.

You may have conformed to outside pressures to do things that were inappropriate—things you would never do today—out of feelings of abandonment, neglect, or abuse at home. Perhaps you felt the only way out of your painful existence was to succumb to value systems that ended up being detrimental and destructive.

Those old, destructive values that you embraced when you were in pain no longer resonate with your true essence. The negativity they brought into your life served no useful purpose. The Law of Sobriety reminds you that to reduce the negativity in your life, you must align yourself with your authentic nature. By changing your values to match your genuine character, you generate the positive energy required to attract people and a way of life that matches your true vibration, and a life of peace and serenity will become possible.

When your energy field is filled with negativity, your quality of life is minimized and it becomes more difficult to take the action steps needed to live the life you truly desire. Mental health professionals say the emotional development of alcoholics and addicts is stunted from the time they begin using; although a person entering rehab is chronologically an adult, developmentally he or she is the age at which substance abuse began.

In the 1940s, psychiatrist Dr. Harry M. Tiebout was an early pioneer in coupling the principles and philosophy of Alcoholics Anonymous with what psychiatrists knew at the time about alcoholism. He characterized alcoholics as egocentric, rebellious against restrictions, preoccupied with a search for pleasure, having feelings of entitlement and omnipotence, unable to accept frustration, displaying a faulty logic, and being markedly irresponsible and immature. Later studies found that alcoholics have trouble recognizing and categorizing emotions in others, and that this problem persists even after they embrace sobriety.

Their values and attitudes at the time addicts and alcoholics began using or drinking support this immature behavior—and often it is these same values and attitudes that led them into addiction in the first place (although, of course, there may be other reasons as well, such as family trauma and genetic predisposition). The Law of Sobriety says that only when the newly sober person grows and transforms, eliminating these immature values, can the positive energy of the universe provide them with the joys of recovery.

WHAT ARE YOUR VALUES?

Your values are what you personally value. I know that sounds like I'm talking in circles, but it's important to remove that overtone of social judgment we often associate with values—that you should have the "right" values or that your personal values should conform to society's values. Your values are uniquely yours. Your personal values are what you stand for and what you would be willing to defend. They are what guide you toward taking action.

Our values change based on when and where we live and who we associate with. Sociologists have long noted that different societies embrace different values. For example, self-sufficiency is regarded as a virtue in some cultures, while other cultures value a person's ability to live as part of a collective society. Social values also change over time. In Shakespeare's day, people thought a public execution was great entertainment and brought their children to watch. Our values about that have certainly changed!

Different groups within a society might also embrace different values. Imagine being a hippie in San Francisco in the 1960s; your values would be very different from those of a police officer living in the same city at the same time. A group of teachers might value being able to communicate effectively and motivate young people. A group of drug addicts might value a person's ability to panhandle effectively and commit crimes without getting caught. A group of athletes might value physical strength, speed, and stamina, while a group of scientists might not find this to be important at all. So values are more of a process than a destination—there is no finality to your values. They can change as your life changes. In your sobriety, your values should make you feel energized, connected, excited, and full of life. Your personal values are like a road map that guides you in the right direction; like a road map you'd use to find your way to an unfamiliar town, the values you embrace in sobriety should help you find your way to your new life.

Our values describe how we see ourselves—our deepest commitments, the ground from which our actions spring.
—From *Falling Awake: Creating the Life of Your Dreams*
by Dave Ellis

Your personal values enable you to stay grounded in what is most important to you, so that when you must make decisions, you have a basis to determine the best approach to take. For example, if a relationship you're in is a trigger to use, if it's causing you distress and you value peace and serenity, this relationship is no longer a fit with your new values in sobriety. You can see that values have nothing to do with feelings or emotions—the action comes first, based on your values, and the feelings follow. If you decided to party last night and miss work this morning, how you feel about your choice will be a result of whether or not the action you took aligned with your values. If you have values that are rooted in your essence—the core of who you are and what you truly believe—your life is not some random set of actions that have no significance. Instead, your life moves in a purposeful direction, and the decisions you make lead you to your goals.

WHY VALUES CHANGE

The Law of Sobriety is all about living on purpose and with meaning, and that is a direct result of the values you live by. Your values cannot be clarified until you feel whole and have resolved past issues or traumas. It is important to realize that you're not stuck in the past. You have a choice: Do you want to live a life that nurtures sobriety, or do you want to live your life the way you have always lived it? Members of the twelve-step fellowship call living as you have always lived "insanity." Insanity is doing the same thing over and over again and expecting different results. That just doesn't make sense. And that's why values must always be evolving.

It's obvious that if you are trying to get clean and sober, the adolescent values you clung to so many years ago no longer work for you as an adult. The old value that you must fit in at any cost is no longer a match to the person you are becoming. The value of being willing to do anything just to be accepted as part of a group no longer aligns with your value to be clean and sober. You need to embrace values that move you forward rather than backward.

The world is full of people that have stopped listening to themselves or have listened only to their neighbors to learn what they ought to do, how they ought to behave, and what the values are they should be living for.

—From *The Power of Myth* by Joseph Campbell

What constitutes a good value system? Certainly, there are core values that are part of a meaningful, sober lifestyle. Some of those values are listed in the box below. But other values change as we change. Maybe when you were sixteen years old, your most important value was to fit in with your peers. At twenty, it might have been to hang out at the hippest clubs in your city. At thirty, maybe it was to get a high-paying job. There's nothing wrong with valuing any of those things. Good values are those that resonate with who you are *at that moment* in your life. You know your values are good and right for you because they resonate with who you truly are.

> ## What Do You Value?
> Values are unique to each of us and keep changing as we change. Many people who are living a life that's in tune with the Law of Sobriety have found the following values resonate with them.
> * Accountability
> * Appreciation
> * Authenticity
> * Creativity
> * Dependability
> * Focus
> * Generosity
> * Honesty
> * Patience
> * Self-reliance
> * Tolerance
> * Willingness to explore

Changing values follow the essence of the Zen principle known as "beginner's mind." Shunryu Suzuki, a Japanese Zen priest who popularized Zen Buddhism in the United States, wrote in *Zen Mind, Beginner's Mind*, "If your mind is empty, it is always ready for anything; it is open to everything. In the beginner's mind there are many possibilities. In the expert's mind there are few." In other words, the expert's mind has already decided everything and cannot change. The beginner's mind is always learning and changing. As this applies to values, it means that with a beginner's mind, you can always change your values to meet your new life purpose.

Obviously, your values as a recovering alcoholic or addict are going to be different from those you held when you were abusing substances. Addicts value the ability to avoid emotional pain. In sobriety, you value being able to walk through pain. The twelve-step fellowship reminds us "to not pick up a drink no matter what." You always have the power to choose to pick up that first drink or not, even when life is throwing its worst at you. But after that first drink, you are powerless. Being true to the values you have embraced in your sobriety means you need never again be powerless in your recovery.

You are called upon to think for yourself, to believe in yourself, and to consciously create a peaceful and sustainable version of reality by accepting complete responsibility for your life.

—From *Path of Empowerment*
by Barbara Marciniak

The Law of Sobriety is about being more purposeful and less random, more powerful and less impotent. It is based on the concept that if you are willing to put your energy into sobriety, that same energy will come back to you—and you will reap the rewards. The Law of Sobriety is grounded in accountability for your actions. Your actions and the consequences of them are not the results of chance or luck, but rather are a direct result of the values you live by and believe in. If you are not living a life that is true to your values, there is a good chance that you feel dissatisfied, depressed, angry, frustrated, and fearful. If you are not living in alignment with your core values, you will have very little energy to pursue what you desire in your relationships, work, spiritual life, health and well-being, and, of course, recovery.

You might want to ask yourself why you are feeling restless, burned-out, frustrated, complacent, or in a rut. Are you living a life that honors who you are or who you are becoming? If not, what is blocking you from living out your core values? Maybe you don't know how to access what your true values are. This is when the Law of Sobriety can be a conduit to discovering them.

Consider that perhaps this is not the time to direct the show, but to ask the universe to handle the details and trust that the answers will come. The exercises at the end of this chapter will help you do that. Sometimes in those still moments of silence, we discover the answers from that small voice inside that we call intuition.

The gift of intuition is the insight you need, that your worldly rational mind can't pick up. Intuition is God's mind flowing through you, so that you get the real facts. The real Truth.

—From *Thinking from the Infinite*
by Carell Zaehn

FINDING YOUR TRUE VALUES

It's important to remember that the Law of Sobriety says your values must align with your true essence to produce the positive energy it will take to attract everything in life that you desire. When you realize which aspects of your life are working and which are not, your truth will be revealed to you, and the universe will respond accordingly.

Tools for Change
Thinking About Your Values

When thinking about your values, it can be helpful to imagine yourself in the future as the person you wish to become. When you look at that person, you can think about what values that person has. Remember, when you are positive and really believe this is the person you are becoming, the Law of Sobriety will help you make it happen.

- Take a piece of paper and list people you know who are in recovery and who have values you admire.
- List the values they have that align with yours.
- Imagine yourself one year, five years, and ten years from now, and write down how you see yourself living in terms of your personal relationships, health and well-being, prosperity, spiritual growth, and recovery plan. Don't define yourself by what you do for a living, but by who you want to become as a person.
- Make a list of the actions you are willing to take to become that person you want to be.
- Ask yourself what the barriers are to attaining a value-driven sobriety.
- Think about whether the values you believe in today match with your sobriety goals.
- Make a list of strategies you will need to take to live in alignment with your values. Write down daily steps, weekly steps, monthly steps, and yearly steps. These small steps will not only help you achieve your goal in bite-size pieces, but will also align you with your value to live a life of health and well-being. Remember, it's the small steps that make up the big picture. For example, perhaps a long-term goal is to lose twenty pounds. That's a big, perhaps overwhelming task. So break it down into small steps: today you will use the stairs instead of the escalator at the mall; this week you

will do some gardening rather than hiring someone to do it for you; this month you will talk to your doctor about the best way to change your diet. To achieve your goal of sobriety, perhaps this week you will call a new member of your twelve-step meeting to welcome him or her; next month you will become a sponsor or a mentor to a newcomer; next year you will go on vacation with your sober friends.

• Commit to what you are willing to do when your current values clash with your recovery. If your ultimate goal is to remain sober and you value a sober lifestyle, you must commit to taking the necessary steps to remain sober. If you know hanging around with buddies who are still using is a trigger into relapse, you must stop socializing with them—even if loyalty to friends is something you value. If you know going out for coffee with other sober people after a twelve-step meeting aligns with your value to develop a circle of sober friends, you must take the actions to attain that goal. It's just that simple.

When your values align with your true essence, you are doing the things you are good at and truly enjoy. We all have unique talents. When your gifts are manifested in your life, you will feel whole, complete, and fulfilled. It's important to remember that not all gifts involve your career or a job. Your special talent may be fostering a happy family life, playing a musical instrument, writing, working in your garden, acting, speaking, being a volunteer, or something else that just "feels right" for you. Your gift comes in a form that authentically expresses who you are. When you find it you will know it, and you must follow that knowing. It will be what brings you the most inner peace, joy, freedom, and exhilaration. It will resonate from the values that you will be most proud of when you look back on your life.

Kim and Donna's Story

A distraught client of mine brought her teenage daughter to see me. My client Kim felt she was losing control of her daughter, who Kim suspected was using drugs. Her daughter, Donna, was once a cheerleader and an A student, but had started hanging around with a questionable group of friends, isolating herself from her family and former friends, and acting out when she was at home.

Although seeking advice is important, Kim discussed her daughter's every negative attribute with many other people: her own friends, the school guidance counselor, and anyone else willing to listen to a worried mother. Not once did she talk about Donna's positive qualities. Of course, her daughter needed direction, but she also needed to be encouraged to embrace activities that represented her core values, such as her creativity and sensitivity to others. Donna was embracing behaviors and values that did not align with her true self, and the negative energy was rushing in. Kim's constant negativity was not helping things.

Psychologists have confirmed something that our great-great-grandparents already knew: you catch more flies with honey than you do with vinegar. Pioneering research by psychologist Sidney Bijou in the 1950s and '60s showed that positive reinforcement is the best way to encourage positive behavior in children, and that punishment—verbal or physical—does not have a positive effect on children's behavior. One of his most famous studies revealed that if a teacher simply paid attention to a child when he was well behaved and ignored him when he was disruptive, the child's behavior would quickly improve.

I suggested ways Kim could approach the situation with her daughter in a more positive way. She enrolled Donna in an art class, and the daughter's positive energy quickly expanded. When Donna's activities were aligned with her true values, the universe offered opportunities that enabled her to thrive. Values represent the commitments that guide your choices and ultimately determine the quality of your life. Once Kim's daughter aligned her life with her values of being imaginative, inventive, and nurturing toward others, she had no need to hang around with people who were dragging her down. When she surrounded herself with people and activities that resonated with her authentic values, negative actions and influences no longer seemed so seductive, because Donna was doing what made her truly happy at her core. In accordance with the Law of Sobriety, the universe then gave her the energy to move away from what was negative in her life.

A Life Rooted in Values

When I worked in hospice, which is end-of-life care, I counseled the patients and families as they were going through the process of dying and anticipatory grieving. In my experience, the patients who were rooted in their spirituality had a much easier time of going through the dying process. They felt an overwhelming peace that all was okay and that this was their time. They accepted it without an emotional struggle, even when they were in physical pain.

People who work in hospice care often say that patients die as they lived. Nothing could be more true when we lose loved ones from the disease of alcoholism or addiction. Their deaths are a direct result of how they chose to live their lives.

I remember one particular hospice patient who was also in recovery. I went to visit her, met her husband (who also was newly sober), and was greeted by a roomful of their closest friends from the twelve-step program. Their friends had brought much more than food and flowers; they brought with them enough faith to carry this beautiful couple through the painful process of dying and watching someone you love take her last breath. I was so moved by this experience. It will always remind me of how the values of faith and fellowship helped this woman make the transition to the other side in one of the most meaningful passings I have ever witnessed.

One way to unearth your values is to ask yourself some questions: What are the moments in my life that are especially fulfilling or rewarding? When do I notice a surge of energy that shifts me from hopelessness to hope? From deep-seated pain to peace? From despair to a relentless drive? Who am I with, or am I alone? What am I doing at that moment?

Once you have identified those moments in your life, ask yourself, when did I allow my fearful voice to talk me out of making a choice that honored my values? We all have that inner voice that wants to keep us from following our dreams. There are many names for it: the inner critic, negative self-talk, the committee, the program. This voice wants you to believe your dreams are silly, impossible, ludicrous, insane, doomed to fail. That same voice is the one that tells you, "You can't stay sober." Yes, this voice is out to get you. It wants you to judge and criticize yourself. It wants to kill your hope. The Law of Sobriety will help get you to a place where you can silence—or at least ignore—that inner critic.

My Own Story

I had such a moment, a moment when I reconnected with my values, about two years ago. I was sitting in a staff meeting at a rehab center in Malibu, where I had worked for only three months. The owner of the center called on me to discuss a patient's case, asking what her discharge plans were. The patient was a mother of three young children and had been in rehab for almost three months. She was missing her children tremendously, and her husband was failing to cope effectively with the stress of child care.

As a rehab professional, I know that the longer a person stays in treatment, the better their chances for recovery. The average time a patient stays in treatment is thirty days, but ninety days increases the chances of a better outcome. Still, it was my professional opinion that her family needed her. So I recommended she return home, attend an outpatient treatment program, go to twelve-step meetings, and continue in one-on-one psychotherapy.

The clinic owner would hear nothing of it. He believed she needed to stay and insisted that I tell her husband that if she didn't stay, "She will die." The problem was that I did not believe it was true. I knew this woman was needed somewhere else and that if she stayed at the treatment center, it might even set back her recovery. I believed sending her home with a solid plan to deal with her recovery was the best treatment plan for this patient, who was not just a "recovering alcoholic" but also a wife and mother. At that point, I knew I needed to leave that job. The values of that rehab center no longer aligned with mine. If I stayed one minute longer, I would be denying what I stood for.

In fact, I had always wanted to set up my own private practice. But my inner critic always reminded me that if I tried, there would be no other income out there to support me. Fear of losing the security of a steady job and doubts about my ability to support myself on my own had always immobilized me and had kept me from pursuing my dream. But at that moment, when my boss demanded I do something that went against my values, I realized there were no other options for me. If I wanted to remain true to myself, then it was time to move on.

I quit my job and pursued my private practice full time. Because I was aligned with my true values, positive energy flowed into me and I was determined to make it work no matter what. I was finally able to pursue what I had gone to graduate school for: to help people and do it in a way that brought out the best in me, both personally and professionally. I was on my way to living my truth. Living in fear and negativity was no longer an option.

MOVING BEYOND NEGATIVITY

Negativity is the hallmark of addictive thinking. A negative belief system may stem from growing up in an unsafe environment, which sets you up for a mind-set that can ultimately lead to thinking of yourself as a perpetual victim. The victim blames others for all his problems, rather than looking inside himself and taking responsibility for his behavior. A series of disappointments can also lead to a victim mentality, where you come to believe you will never get what you deserve.

Adding fear to that equation is what makes addiction so "cunning, baffling, and powerful." (That's how the *Alcoholics Anonymous Big Book*, the cornerstone text of twelve-step programs, describes it, and I think it's quite accurate.) Fear is what makes addicts dependent. When you feel it is never enough—whatever that "it" is—you become frozen in fear. You can't change and you can't move forward.

If you grew up in a dysfunctional home, you probably focused on giving others what they needed from you, just as a way to survive. You learned to be "other" focused. This focus can transfer into your relationships with people outside your family, so how you feel about yourself is based on how others view you. You will always be in fear because there is always the possibility that others are not going to validate you, and this fear will keep you stuck in negativity and your addiction. This fear is also why you try to manipulate everything and everyone around you, believing in the illusion that you are in control because you felt so out of control as a child.

Negative thinking is an energy drain that cuts us off from our life force and hastens us toward a nonliving state. Rather than seeing the possibilities within and around us, we see only our limitations and the things we cannot do.

—From *When Society Becomes an Addict*
by Anne Wilson Schaef

It's time to let go of the values you learned from your parents or caregivers that are keeping you down. Just because they were fearful people or they were not there for you doesn't mean you need to make their negativity a part of your life. Even if they made you feel the world was an unstable, unsafe place, the Law of Sobriety says you are free to choose your own set of values, right now.

If substance abuse is interfering with your desires and you keep behaving in self-destructive ways, you are allowing your addictions to become more important than your true values. Avoiding what is difficult never works out because, in the end, you are selling out yourself and what you value most—just as for me, staying at that treatment center would have been selling out myself.

Being negative can be addictive and, in some peculiar way, comforting. It enables you to see yourself as a victim and avoid taking responsibility for changing your life. It allows you to not move forward, not align with your values, not follow your passions, not even discover what those passions are. It allows you to stay in your disease and not even take the first baby steps toward fulfillment. You may even believe that if you are negative enough, you are protecting yourself from disappointment or will be able to handle whatever comes your way. But the Law of Sobriety says it is the negativity itself that brings you exactly what you *don't* want.

The Law of Sobriety works when you are optimistic and have a positive state of mind. Pessimists are immobilized by fear. Their options seem few, and they are cut off by their own negative energy, resonating the worst possible outcome. They say things like, "I will never get that job," "She will never go out with me," "How can I possibly make new, clean and sober friends?" or "I will never be accepted." Optimists radiate hope and see possibilities even in the most difficult situations.

The negative way of thinking always asks, "When am I going to get mine?" But it also keeps reminding, "Good things never come to me." It is a push and pull of "I don't deserve anything because I am nothing, but I deserve everything because of what I didn't get." When you get stuck in this confusing way of thinking, your mind will take the smallest shred of truth and turn it upside down and inside out, so that you never even get a chance to begin what you are truly called to do. This is the time to ask yourself what it is you are resisting. What are you doing to avoid your truth?

When we honor our values, we feel an internal "rightness." It's as if each value produces its own special tone. When we live our values, the various tones create a unique harmony.

—From *Co-Active Coaching* by L. Whitworth, et al.

Guided Visualization

Guided visualization is a kind of meditation in which you listen to a voice that leads your imagination on a journey. The purpose of the journey may be to achieve healing. It will help you achieve deep relaxation and release. It will also allow you to reflect on important questions and become aware of the answers to those questions.

Negative emotions or beliefs prevent you from realizing that the answers to these questions lie within you. As your conscious mind follows the imaginary journey, experiences come forward to be acknowledged and released from your subconscious. This enables you to become more positive in your contemplation.

When you do a guided visualization, you sit or lie down in a relaxed position and listen to a recorded script. You can buy a CD or listen to a guided visualization online. You can also find scripts online and in books (or write your own) and record them yourself. (Some people don't like the sound of their own voice and ask a friend to record the script for them.)

A guided visualization may last from five to forty-five minutes and typically is meant to achieve a particular goal, such as answering a question, letting go of something negative, or healing a physical or emotional wound. One great advantage of guided visualization is that even if you fall asleep, you still benefit subconsciously.

You may find that you prefer different scripts at different times. Just find what works best for you. When you are shopping for guided visualization CDs, see if you can listen to a brief passage first, so you have an idea of whether that particular script resonates with you. Guided visualization CDs may also be called guided meditation or yoga nidra. For a list of some suggested CDs and Internet resources, please see the Resources section at the end of the book.

EMBRACING CHANGE

I have had many clients who resist going to rehab, both because they are not ready to become clean and sober and because they are in absolute terror of "being away" for thirty days. Fear of the unknown cripples them. They resist even the smallest step toward change because on some level they don't believe they will succeed. They tell themselves that they can get sober "alone," even though time and time again they try and cannot. They sabotage themselves by allowing their negative voices to run the show. Even when there is a smidgen of hope that they can get sober this time, the inner critic comes back with a resounding "No, you can't do it."

If you are struggling with a similar decision, maybe it's time to heed Mahatma Gandhi's words of wisdom: "Live as if you were to die tomorrow. Learn as if you were to live forever." Don't move away from something hopeful because you are afraid or you feel uncomfortable. Remember, you don't have to feel confident to act according to what you value. If you are scared, it's okay; do it anyway. In Chapter 2, I talked about the idea of acting "as if." Act as if you are not afraid. Be clear about your values and take the action steps to align yourself with what is important to you. When you do, the Law of Sobriety says positive energy will crowd out the negativity and fear that have held you back for too long.

Tools for Change
Living in Harmony with Your Values

This guided visualization will help you clarify your values and live a life that is in harmony with what's important to you. Rather than listening to a voice guide you through this experience, you can just imagine these scenarios as you breathe. Or, if you like, you can record your own voice guiding you and then play it back to do this exercise.

- Spend ten to twenty minutes a day just breathing. Take full breaths deep into your belly and notice what arises in your body during each moment of inhalation and exhalation. Think of things that are already in your life that make it worth living and notice how these thoughts affect your body and your breathing.
- Take a moment to greet the recovering addict or alcoholic in you with compassion and ask it what resentments, fears, and concerns are preventing you from identifying your values and reaching your goals. Take a moment to speak to the part of you that values the truth and the part of you that is lying to yourself. Speak to them separately, so you understand the difference in their messages. Ask yourself if you are going to let your life be driven by your values or by your addictions. Now, thank that part of you that has told the truth, has let go of your addictions, and is ready to embark on the journey of recovery with an innate understanding of what a meaningful life looks like for you.
- Imagine yourself standing on the shore of a vast ocean. Your feet feel the sand gently wash over them as a wave rolls in, then the sand pulls away as the wave rolls out. You hear only the sound of the moving water. Notice what this image feels like throughout your body in all your senses. Visualize where you want to be in your life one year, five years, ten years from now—without any limitations. Breathe the sea air and just notice what comes up for you.

Now that you are seeing yourself where you want to be, begin to ask yourself the following questions by closing your eyes, breathing in the questions, and breathing out the answers.

✓ What is the landscape?

✓ What am I wearing?

✓ Am I alone? If not, who is with me?

✓ What does my life's work look like?

✓ What type of intimate relationship am I in?

✓ Am I a parent?

✓ Am I in school?

✓ What type of friends and social life do I have?

✓ How is my health and well-being?

✓ What is my relationship like with my higher power or the universe?

✓ What do I have faith in?

✓ What am I contributing to the universe?

✓ How do I play and have fun?

✓ What will my legacy be?

• Feel yourself attuned to your true self, right now, in this very moment. See that there are no limits to the dreams you have for yourself. Know in your deepest being that as long as you are in recovery, there is nothing in the way of you discovering your true values and reaching the goals you set.

• Once you have answered these questions, create several affirmations that will help you clarify and be in harmony with your values. Value affirmations enable you to stay true to your values and move forward, rather than staying stuck in old values that no longer resonate with who you are now. Here are some examples of affirmations related to recovery, but feel free to create your own. Remember, your values are unique and your affirmations should reflect your own path of self-discovery.

✓ My actions align with the values I believe in.

✓ My energy is aligned with the goals I was put on Earth to accomplish.

✓ I value my recovery program because it moves me closer to my higher power, the universe, and a spiritual way of living.

✓ I no longer use fear as a way to avoid pursuing my dreams.

✓ My values honor my sobriety by staying away from people, places, and things that are triggers.

✓ I value taking care of my body, my mind, and my spirit.

✓ I value fun and enjoy myself in my recovery.

✓ I value being a part of a recovery community.

✓ I value feeling connected to the friends and family in my life.

✓ I value enlightening others about my journey in recovery.

✓ My energy flows in the direction of my values.

FOUR

Living a Life of Authenticity

There is a simple universal principle:
Everything in the universe wants to be accepted.
All aspects of creation want to be loved
and appreciated and included. So, any quality or energy
you are not allowing yourself to experience
or express will keep coming up inside you, or around you,
until you recognize it as a part of you, until you accept it
and integrate it into your personality and your life.
—From *The Path of Transformation*
by Shakti Gawain

Authenticity is about being honest, especially with yourself, in everything you think, say, and do. When you are living authentically, the energy of who you are on the inside will be expressed on the outside, according to the Law of Sobriety. Behaving in an authentic manner is the only way for your true self to emerge. If you have spent years lying and hiding from yourself, this may not be easy for you. What you need to remember is that not living a life of authenticity carries a very high cost, while living in your truth brings huge benefits. When you are using drugs or alcohol, you get caught up in a vortex of lying to yourself and everyone around you. In some situations, lying may seem easier than telling the truth. But hiding your truth makes you defensive, fearful, angry, shameful, and unwilling to change. If you can escape the vortex of lying and access who you really are, the Law of Sobriety says you will awaken to your true nature. No matter what the circumstances, you will be aligned with your true self. This is what it means to live a life of authenticity.

THE FALSE SELF

Alcoholics and addicts often come from dysfunctional families, or they have inherited a genetic disposition to become alcoholics and addicts, which means they have parents or other relatives who have the disease. When parents are alcoholics or drug addicts, they are not physically or emotionally present for their children. This type of neglect is quite common in the families of addicts, and the result is traumatized children.

Families in which the parents are addicts are built around shame and secrets. The family may look normal from the outside, but inside, chaos prevails. Children from these families collude with the secret that "everything is okay," because the family may turn against any member who tries to bring attention to the problem. These children wear masks on the outside so they don't jeopardize the "family secret" that their parents are alcoholics, drug addicts, abusive, or neglectful.

Children in this situation develop a false self as a way to hide the dysfunction of their family or to deny to themselves how sick their family really is. They often slip into this false self unconsciously, and their true self never has an opportunity to emerge. Psychiatrist Karen Horney wrote about what happens when these children grow up in her book *Neurosis and Human Growth*. She said adult children of alcoholics may continue living within this role because it seems easier and safer, but it comes at a terrible price: honesty, authenticity, and a clear sense of identity are sacrificed. Eventually, the adult children of alcoholics become the false personas they have created and end up out of touch with who they really are. Their fear of exposing the family makes them cling to their false self at any cost. There is such anxiety about what might happen if the "shameful family secret" ever got out that their true self remains hidden away—not to be revealed until years later.

Parents who are caught up in their own problems and dysfunction leave little room for their children to know who they are, how they feel, or what they want. The children are truly invisible to these unavailable parents. There are no opportunities for them to discover their true essence because they are too busy taking care of their parents' needs. They become children who have to act like adults way before their time, leaving very few opportunities to have hopes, dreams, and aspirations of their own.

In some cases, these children become addicts or alcoholics themselves. Through their own recovery process, they begin to uncover their true self after years of hiding who they really are and what they have been through. Others may not become addicts or alcoholics, but still carry a great deal of shame from their family experiences. They become codependent, trying to please everyone and everything while abandoning their own needs and desires.

Dominique's Story

If someone is living with a false identity, how can their authentic self ever become apparent? Dominique's family, friends, and coworkers viewed her as a very controlling person. Any spontaneity she might have had was overshadowed by her need to always have a plan for everything. Her husband once tried to surprise her with a weekend getaway, but she became angry rather than delighted. She could not cope with any surprises, no matter how big or small.

To the people around Dominique, this type of behavior seemed controlling. But in fact, when she encountered the unexpected, she became immobilized with anxiety. When she was growing up, chaos reigned at home. Both her parents were addicts, and there were no boundaries in Dominique's home. Everything changed around her all the time and in unpredictable ways. There were no rules. There were no bedtime rituals, family dinners, homework schedules, or anything else that might have given Dominique the structure every child needs to feel safe and secure. Therefore, having things she could count on—things she could anticipate and plan for—meant everything to Dominique. She craved the stability and safety of sameness. Change did not feel safe, and she avoided it at all costs.

Dominique's authentic, spontaneous self was blocked by her need to maintain control in every area of her life so that she would never be taken by surprise. Everything had to be preplanned. She was also very serious; she did not know how to relax and just have fun. The childlike part of Dominique was never part of her conscious reality. She could not attract joy in her life because she was always putting her need for control and rigidity out to the universe. A life devoid of spontaneity and delight was what she got back.

With her childlike self so subdued, the only way Dominique could relax was with alcohol. It was only when she was drunk that she could keep her immobilizing fear of chaos at bay and let her inner child come out and play. Dominique had childhood trauma she was not dealing with and a rigid, inauthentic adult persona that was not bringing her happiness. It was only when she lifted up her mask during the recovery process that she was able to see who she really was.

The Law of Sobriety can help uncover your lost inner child by attracting back the happiness you once had—perhaps a very long time ago—and that your false self has stolen from you. Working through the steps of the Law of Sobriety enables you to recover what was taken away from you during those early developmental years. It allows you to uncover the lost energy of your original, true self; the self who has always been there, hidden from you and the world.

This life force or energy had been trapped within Dominique because she had been developmentally too young to process the chaos that was going on in her family. Her alcoholism was a way for her to self-medicate enough to relax the grip of fear and release just a tiny bit of the positive energy that had been trapped in her unconscious. When she became aware of these feelings during the recovery process, the Law of Sobriety helped Dominique unearth a sense of wholeness and happiness that had eluded her for decades. The fear and chaos she had internalized as a child had kept her in the disease of alcoholism as an adult. But that way of behaving no longer resonated with the person she wanted to become.

THE REPETITION TRAP

Another consequence of having a history of trauma is the continuation of behaviors that go against your authentic self and your value system. You know these behaviors do not resonate with your true self, and yet you fall into the trap of repeating them anyway. A client of mine illustrates this point.

April's Story

April was discharged from the rehab center where I was working. She decided she would not date for at least the first six months of her sobriety. She knew dating and alcohol always went together for her—

drinking was a way to cope with the anxiety of being with someone new. She also knew in her innermost being that if she became intoxicated, she would compromise her moral values and would end up having sex without a second thought. Her authentic self was not the kind of person who hopped into bed so readily, but her false self was. Yet, instead of going to twelve-step meetings, April decided to join a dating service soon after she was discharged from rehab, and she began serial dating. April could not be alone, and the only way she knew how to fill up her insatiable emptiness was to either drink or cling to any man who might show interest in her—even if that interest was solely sexual. Before long, she was drinking on her dates and sexually acting out again.

By going against the Law of Sobriety, April used all her energy pretending to be someone she wasn't, and this ultimately brought her back to drinking. Her behaviors were in conflict with her true self. She was not taking responsibility for her choices. April's promiscuous behavior was an unconscious way to get the love and acceptance she was longing for but never had. But instead of love, all she felt was shame and guilt—the same feelings she'd had as a child. April said she wanted a healthy relationship, but her behavior sent out a different message.

Our work together involved uncovering her suppressed feelings. April had felt "unlovable" as a child, and together we explored how that manifested in her adult relationships. The goal was to help April feel accepted. She finally realized that for her, that meant no more serial dating. Instead, she turned to twelve-step meetings for support.

One of the sayings in a twelve-step fellowship is, "We will love you until you love yourself." For April, the power of that acceptance in an atmosphere where there was no alcohol and no sex helped her break out of her cycle of repetitive, negative behavior. She was then in a position to work through the healing process. Learning how to separate her adult needs from her childhood needs (what therapists call "the corrective experience") continued to be part of April's recovery process. She realized that she needed more time to develop coping skills so she wouldn't feel the need to drink when dating. There was another very important component to her recovery. April had to develop profound compassion for herself to stop her self-destructive behaviors. Once April began accepting herself and participating in activities that matched her authentic being, she was able to put the Law of Sobriety to work. She understood she was not quite ready for a healthy relationship, so she started volunteering, painting, and doing yoga. These activities brought her joy because they were authentic expressions of who she truly was. She was finally being honest with herself, and she incorporated this authenticity into her everyday existence.

There is no desire that anyone holds for any other reason than that they believe they will feel better in the achievement of it. Whether it is a material object, a physical state of being, a relationship, a condition, or a circumstance—at the heart of every desire is the desire to feel good. And so, the standard of success is absolutely the amount of joy you feel.

—From *Ask and It is Given:*
Learning to Manifest Your Desires
by Esther and Jerry Hicks

Traumatized individuals often fall into the repetition trap in another way, too: they recreate their trauma by repeating unhealthy relationships over and over again. This is known as a cycle of reenactment or repetition. Sigmund Freud wrote about this phenomenon in 1920, observing that people tend to repeat the emotional, psychological, or behavioral aspects of a traumatic event over and over again. One way they do so is by putting themselves in situations where similar events are likely to happen again. According to Freud (and later psychologists as well), people tend to recreate circumstances in their lives that they feel are unresolved. It's a desperate attempt to undo or fix the trauma they experienced early in life. They believe that if they can "just get it right," the emotional pain they have carried with them throughout their lives will finally be exorcised. Of course, this never works, and they end up getting into one abusive relationship after another, because they do not know how to set boundaries in their relationships.

If you aren't consciously aware of absorbing someone else's energy, pay closer attention to your vibes and then ask yourself if they are, in fact, your vibes. The depression or anxiety you're feeling may not really be your own; it may be the result of absorbing too much of what's around you.

—From *Trust Your Vibes*
by Sonia Choquette

RELATIONSHIP BOUNDARIES

Setting your own personal boundaries is an important part of living authentically. Boundaries in a relationship can be described as the space between where you end and the other person begins. Boundaries can refer to actual physical space, but also to psychological space; when psychological space is not respected, jealousy or possessiveness are typical results. Boundaries allow us to say no so that others don't infiltrate our sense of self. Unhealthy relationships often have no boundaries. The purpose of boundaries is not to limit yourself, but to take care of yourself. When you set boundaries, you protect yourself from inappropriate behavior (both your own behavior and the behavior of others) so you will not feel victimized.

In dysfunctional family systems, there may be no boundaries—and if there are, they are often broken. Children in these families don't learn about boundaries early in life. As an adult, it's very difficult to adhere to healthy boundaries if you don't even know what they look like. Some of the more common relationship boundaries that addicts and alcoholics overstep include extremes of attachment: they either get too close and fused with another person or remain distant and disengaged from that person. Drug addicts and alcoholics are often confused as to what an appropriate relationship looks like. They tend to be either too trusting or not trusting at all. Their relationships end up being either too intense and dependent, or too detached because there is no real commitment.

The too-intense type of relationship usually ends up being abusive, either physically, emotionally, or psychologically. Without healthy boundaries in place, these relationships have an addictive quality right from the start. Addicts become overly attached to other people and let themselves be taken advantage of. They are over compliant, always saying yes when they mean no. They don't know what it means to be respected. They don't know when or how to end a destructive relationship. They don't know what they have a right to ask for. They are deathly afraid of losing the relationship, so they feel they must always be the one who gives in.

These relationships do not have any of the flexibility, security, and sense of safety found in a healthy relationship. Unclear or nonexistent boundaries lead to toxic attempts to be loved even when the relationship is unsafe. People who have grown up being invisible crave being seen, even if it is in a negative light. They are so afraid of being abandoned that they cannot leave, even when they know the relationship is dangerous physically, emotionally, or psychologically.

To find your true self within a relationship, you must always determine where you draw the line in terms of what is acceptable behavior, communicate that to the other person, and clearly spell out the consequences if your boundaries are not respected. Then you must follow through and stick to the consequences you have outlined—even if it means leaving the relationship. You *can* find someone better, and you will. I know this from personal experience.

My Own Story

When I was growing up, my parents used to fight a lot about money. My parents were very loving—to each other and to me and my brother—most of the time. But when they were angry with each other, you knew it. Their anger was out of proportion to the events they were reacting to, and when they fought, they said hurtful things to each other. They had their own frustrations. My mom worked full-time, and it was unusual in those days for mothers to have a job outside of the home. But our family needed the income. I know this was quite stressful for her because she would much rather have stayed home with my brother and me. I think it was stressful for my father, too, because on some level he felt he wasn't living up to his potential or earning enough to enable my mom to stay at home.

Their fighting traumatized me as a young child. I remember trying to escape the unbearable screaming that went on around me by making up soap opera stories in my head. Certainly, I had no idea what healthy boundaries looked like in terms of what people in a relationship say to each other. When I became a young adult, I found myself in relationships where verbal abuse was the norm. I attracted men who would yell, insult, criticize, and control me, and who were emotionally unavailable. The abuse tore at my self-esteem. And yet, these men could be very loving and supportive. It was quite chaotic and confusing to me. I would often stay in these unhealthy relationships because I would get sucked in by the parts that made me feel loved and accepted. Unfortunately, it was only a matter of time before the "love" would be replaced by verbal abuse and the cycle would begin all over again.

I always thought I could "fix" these relationships—I could somehow have the loving part of a man without all the abuse—but that never happened. It wasn't until much later in my adult life that I realized I was recreating the kind of relationship I had experienced growing up. My parents did the best they could, but they had unresolved issues from their own childhoods that they re-created in their marriage. And now my relationships duplicated parts of my parents' relationship. This cycle of relationships with unhealthy boundaries was self-perpetuating.

I could not access the energy of the Law of Sobriety because my authentic self was hidden away in fear and shame. When I started making healthier choices about who I associated with—whether they were friendships or intimate relationships—my self-esteem increased. I began to feel empowered after I finished graduate school and was able to work in the field I was passionate about. Eventually, I felt confident enough to begin to set boundaries in my relationships. I knew I deserved to feel healthy, safe, and secure in any relationship, and that is exactly what I attracted once I made the conscious choice to accept nothing less.

As I look back, it upsets me to realize that I allowed myself to endure so much pain for such a large part of my adult life. In my work, I see so many clients who stay in unhealthy, even dangerous, relationships because they fear being alone and never finding anyone else. They will do anything to avoid the emptiness they are terrified of feeling, and they believe it is impossible for them to find someone better. But their unsatisfying relationships leave a void that they fill with anything other than what is best for them—drugs, alcohol, gambling, compulsive shopping, sex addiction, binge eating, and a host of other addictions. They have such feelings of self-hatred, inadequacy, and uselessness that healthy relationships elude them.

You cannot have an authentic sense of yourself until you begin to embody wholeness and truth. Without that, the Law of Sobriety says you will continue to attract self-destructive relationships and compulsive behaviors. You don't wake up one morning with self-esteem. True self-worth comes from the actions you take over time, large or small, that align with your values and your authentic self. The Law of Sobriety can only work when you exhibit self-love and refuse to let toxic people into your life. When you know where to draw the line and then you stand firm, the Law of Sobriety says the universe will attract into your life the healthy people and situations for which you are mentally and spiritually ready.

Relationships based on too much control are not the only ones with unhealthy boundaries. On the other end of the spectrum are people who exhibit detachment, lack of intimacy, distance, and emotional unavailability. Individuals who were not nurtured properly in their developmental years may not have learned to trust their parent or caretaker, and they extend that mistrust to all their relationships. As a result, they retreat when they feel too close to another person, fearing that person will abandon them; they leave the relationship before they are deserted—a result they believe is inevitable. By leaving first, they feel somewhat in control of their emotional life—but they pay a terrible price.

Sean's Story

I have had many clients who say the relationship they're in feels emotionally barren or lacks intimacy. They have no deep connection to the other person, and this often leaves them feeling empty and alone. This is a good description of Sean, who could be considered a serial dater. He found flaws with every woman he went out with. He ran for the hills if he sensed any hint that the other person wanted anything close to a committed relationship.

Although Sean said he wanted to be close to someone, he would back off whenever he started to develop feelings for a woman, complaining about issues with her that really amounted to very small differences. He had trouble maintaining any semblance of a long-term relationship, and instead just ran from one woman to another.

Our work together was for Sean to understand that the insignificant objections he had to these women were really his defense against getting close to them; he avoided closeness because he was afraid of being abandoned all over again, as he was as a child. Sean's parents had divorced when he was very young, and he was raised by his single mother. She spent most of her time working and dating, leaving him alone to care for himself. He finally came to realize that what he truly needed in a relationship was what he was avoiding: a sense of safety, trust, and intimacy.

In therapy Sean was able to redefine what a healthy relationship looks like, and in time he found a very caring, compassionate, loving woman to share his life. Although he would occasionally fear that she might leave him, he was able to walk through this uncertainty and realize his insecurities were just thoughts he had created and did not represent a real threat to his relationship.

Choose to be in close proximity to people who are empowering, who appeal to your sense of connection to intention, who see the greatness in you, who feel connected to God, and who live a life that gives evidence that Spirit has found celebration through them.

—From *The Power of Intention*
by Dr. Wayne Dyer

DENIAL

Denial is one of the biggest and most insidious defense mechanisms that addicts and alcoholics use to convince themselves (and others) they don't have a problem. Their addiction stays alive by swimming in their stream of lies. There is an inner dialogue that goes on in the addict's mind, like a ping-pong match with no winner. One side is dying to use, while the other side begs to be clean and sober. The lies range from "No one will ever know if I just have one drink" to "I am so much more fun when I am high." The healthier side knows the addict has never been able to control his or her drinking and that sobriety is the only way to uncover the more authentic self. But once the lying begins, it's like a cancer that grows out of control. The lying infiltrates every cell in the body and not only affects the addict, but everyone around him or her. The addict can lose his or her home, spouse, children, job, and just about everything else that is important, but an addict will do everything possible to stay in denial and keep the addiction alive.

Christi's Story

When a reality is too delusional, living a life of authenticity is impossible. Christi lost absolutely everything to her addiction in just two

years—her husband, her home, her children, her money. Her denial
ran so deep that she couldn't even see how bad her life had become.
She forgot about the wonderful home life she once had. She cared
nothing for the career, friendships, and stability that had once been so
important to her. No one could convince her she needed help. She
hooked up with a drug dealer and her life tumbled even further down-
hill. She ended up in jail for embezzling money, car theft, and having
illegal drugs in her possession. When she was released from jail, she
started right back up in her cycle of addiction. Even jail wasn't a dark
enough bottom for her to want to get herself clean and sober.

This deep level of denial is debilitating. It takes away your material
life and your family, and robs you of your true self. Your so-called
truth becomes a life of obsessing about drugs, finding ways to obtain
drugs, using drugs, and starting the process all over again. By the time
I saw Christi, she was no longer capable of feeling guilt, remorse, or
shame about her life and how she was hurting herself and those
around her. If those thoughts ever came up, she simply denied them.
She had alienated anyone who had ever loved her or tried to help her.
She had no room for those people in her life because they were trying to take away the thing that was most precious to her, the thing
she lived for: her addiction. She hadn't hit bottom because she was
free-falling in a bottomless pit of denial.

A person in free-fall has two choices. One is to stay in the disease
and keep falling downward to further depths of despair, where you
end up in jail, locked up in an institution, or dead. The other is to
climb up to the path of recovery and recognize your spiritual self.
This is where your authentic nature emerges and you discover the
spiritual being you have always been—and have been denying.

Christi had the choice of two doors to walk through: recovery or
denial. She chose the one that caused her continued destruction and
despair. It was as if the authentic Christi had died and Christi in her

disease was taken over by some malign force. That malign force was her denial; her rationalizations about her situation became her reality. She did not return calls from people she'd met at twelve-step meetings who wanted to support her, because they would also confront her about her behavior. By speaking with them she would have to truly look at herself, which was not something she was ready to do. No one can help an addict or alcoholic unless they are ready to be helped. No one was able to help Christi. As a psychotherapist, I have had to learn that if I am working harder than my clients are willing to work, their recovery is not possible at that time.

AWAKENING TO YOUR AUTHENTIC SELF

Often, spiritual awakening occurs in the midst of chaos or a major crisis. A divorce or a breakup, a death, losing a job, a major move, or an illness may push you too far, and the only way you can get through these life changes is to get help. That certainly happened for me. My divorce, and consequently becoming a single parent, turned my life around. Before then, I was completely lost. My drinking had escalated, and I had an emptiness inside my soul that was so large, only the energy of the universe or a higher power could fill it.

When I started going to AA meetings, the Twelve Steps gave me the tools to begin living again. But my awakening didn't stop there. Eventually, I took a trip to Israel, where many of my relatives live. I had always heard from others who had made the trip that going there is a spiritual experience, where you feel you are part of something much greater than yourself. That's exactly what I needed at the time: I needed to believe in something.

The minute my plane landed, it felt like home. I felt a sense of profound oneness with the country and the people. The trip truly inspired me. When I came back to the United States, I went back to graduate school to become a social worker. I also had a bat mitzvah. This ceremony is a rite of passage in a Jewish person's life in which they assume adult responsibility for their actions in the community. Girls generally have their bat mitzvah at age twelve or thirteen, but I'd never had one, and it was a ritual that said a lot about who and what I wanted to be at that point in my life. (I highly recommend a bar or bat mitzvah or a similar ritual as a way to get in touch with your authentic self; it's never too late.)

These experiences transformed me. Suddenly I wanted to do more than sell advertising for a newspaper (my job at the time). I wanted to help others, especially single parents, and I wanted to make a difference in the world. It was the crisis of being a single parent myself that brought me to my knees, and it was becoming a social worker that changed my world forever. My worst difficulties brought me to my greatest spiritual metamorphosis. Whatever you want to call it—God, higher power, universal energy, Buddha, life force, or collective unconscious—embracing it transformed me, and this transformation gave me the blessing of discovering my authentic self. The Law of Sobriety proved to be true for me, and it can be true for you, too.

Progress, Not Perfection

There's a section in the *Alcoholics Anonymous Big Book* that explains what the Twelve Steps to Recovery are. It also acknowledges that this is not an easy path. The book says, "Many of us exclaimed, 'What an order! I can't go through with it.' Do not be discouraged. No one among us has been able to maintain anything like perfect adherence to these principles. We are not saints. The point is that we are willing to grow along spiritual lines. The principles we have set down are guides to progress. We claim spiritual progress rather than spiritual perfection."

Journaling

If you feel you've fallen out of touch with your authentic self, one way to get back in touch is by journaling. Journaling is more than just keeping a diary; it's a way of exploring the ideas in your conscious and subconscious mind. It can bring into focus your hopes and fears. Journaling about traumatic events can help you explore them and release the emotions associated with them. It can also be a good way to pick your way through problems and find the solutions. Journaling is a tool to help you discover the wisdom that is already within you.

To get started, buy yourself a notebook that you'll use just for your journaling. Buy something you really like. Then set aside a specific time each day when you will write in it. You can even develop a little journaling ritual—you get yourself a cup of tea and sit down at the kitchen table, or you tuck yourself into bed and pick up your journal. Maybe you light a candle first, or put on some special music. Choose a time of day and a ritual that will work for you.

Write the date at the top of the page and just get started. Write for at least ten minutes, or set yourself a page-count goal. Write about whatever pops into your mind. If your mind keeps jumping from subject to subject, let your journal do that, too. Sometimes it can help to write a main idea at the top of a page and then write down anything you think of that is associated with that idea.

Write quickly and don't stop. Don't edit and don't cross out. The key to journaling is to silence your internal editor. Don't worry about whether you're writing well, or gramically, or even coherently. Just write down whatever you think of. If you can't think of anything, write, "I can't think of anything" over and over until something comes to mind.

After you've finished, do something calming for a few minutes. Then come back and read what you just wrote. Try to understand what you have been writing about—what your inner wisdom is trying to tell you. Then write a sentence or two at the bottom of your entry that describes the insight you think you have gained from journaling that day.

You can also go back and reread your journals weeks, months, or even years later. It can be surprising to meet yourself again at the place you were at the moment you wrote each entry. Remember to always read your journal entries with deep compassion for yourself.

What you have refused to experience in a positive way, you will experience in a negative way. If what you are following, however, is your own true adventure, if it is something appropriate to your deep spiritual need or readiness, then magical guides will appear to help you. If you say, "Everyone's going on this trip this year, and I'm going too," then no guides will appear. Your adventure has to be coming right out of your own interior. If you are ready for it, then doors will open where there were no doors before, and where there would not be doors for anyone else.

—From *Reflections on the Art of Living* by Joseph Campbell

The opposite of fear is faith. Finding my spirituality helped me cope more effectively with whatever came my way. And once I knew my authentic self, I stopped living in denial. The abusive relationship I had been in no longer aligned with my essence. My life became enriched and more expansive on so many levels. I made better choices in relationships, I became more present as a mother and a daughter, and I was able to see beyond my own self-centered needs.

My body began to release all the tension that had blocked my energy for more productive and creative things. I was able to manifest as the person I was meant to be. I was able to begin the process of replacing feelings of loss with feelings of love, feelings of anger with feelings of acceptance, feelings of worry with feelings of being worthwhile, and feelings of self-hatred with feelings of self-honoring. No one gave this to me; it came to me from the universal energy that comes with living a life of authenticity. And no one can take it away. It is my choice, and only mine, to either destroy what I have worked so hard to gain or continue to "grow along spiritual lines."

Tools for Change
Uncovering Your Authentic Self

How do you begin to uncover your authentic self? You begin in the stillness of the moment, in a kind of meditation that need not be limited to a particular time of day or a particular amount of time. Just step outside of your usual activities of the day and take a pause. The ideal time for this exercise is ten to twenty minutes, but if you only have five minutes, that's okay.

You can also use this exercise as a coping tool to help center yourself if you are feeling out of balance. Or it can be a way to shift your mood or perceptions. It can also be a sacred time you take in the middle of your day to get out of the hustle and bustle of "doing" and instead slip into just "being."

• Allow yourself to take full breaths in through your nose, deep down into your belly, and out through your mouth. Take four or five of these calming, cleansing breaths. As you breathe, notice your thoughts but don't resist or try to censor any of them. Notice that they are only thoughts and do not need to be judged or acted upon. Just accept them for what they are— thoughts coming and going, nothing more.

• Imagine yourself one year from now. Notice the atmosphere, whether you are alone or with someone else, the colors that surround you, the sky, the ground beneath you, what you are wearing, what you are experiencing with all your senses. When you imagine yourself this way, try to really see who you are. Take some time to explore the parts of yourself that resonate who you truly are and the parts of yourself that are a facade.

• With your eyes gently closed, breathe in the following questions and breathe out the answers:

✓ Am I doing what I need to do in most situations, despite my fears?

✓ Am I aware of my innermost thoughts and feelings?

✓ Am I aware of the filters that hide who I really am?

✓ Do I communicate honestly with myself and others or am I in denial?

✓ Is my behavior aligned with my sobriety?

✓ Do my boundaries align with my true self?

✓ Do I allow my spiritual nature to unfold in my daily living?

• Create in your mind the kind of authenticity that would serve you best. Embody that vision of yourself and trust that this part of you is always there to access. The universe is ready to unleash your true and authentic self.

After completing this exercise, it's time to attract from the universe everything that you are and everything that you are becoming, through daily affirmations. It's important to repeat these affirmations so that you embody and trust their messages. You can even put them on sticky notes around the house, in your car, your office, and any place you are likely to see them every day. When you see the affirmations on the notes, read them to yourself consciously and with awareness, even if you know them by heart. Here are some possibilities.

✓ I am an authentic person and live my life in truth.

✓ I live my life by my belief system and the values that correspond with my beliefs.

✓ I trust the universal energy I put forth in my recovery.

✓ I love the person I am and who I am becoming in sobriety.

✓ I do not live in denial but accept that I am a recovering addict or alcoholic.

✓ My identity is much more than the roles I play.

✓ I set boundaries for myself that keep me safe and away from self-destructive actions.

✓ I no longer hide under a mask of false self-images, but embrace my true self.

The more you repeat these affirmations, the more they will become a part of you. These will be the principles that help guide your journey. Your doubts, fears, and anxieties will lessen because you will know who you are. You will no longer need to be a chameleon, playing different parts depending on who you are with. You will stand grounded in your authenticity.

FIVE.

Learning to Live in Appreciation, Forgiveness, and Compassion

*Compassion, forgiveness, these are the real,
ultimate sources of power for peace and success in life.*
—Tenzian Gyatso, the 14th Dalai Lama

Appreciation, forgiveness, and compassion are interrelated concepts. To live in appreciation means living so that you fully appreciate your life. The Law of Sobriety says you should begin appreciating the gifts of your sober life even if you haven't fully achieved sobriety, because embracing positive change brings more positive change to you. To live your life in appreciation, you must first learn to forgive yourself for your mistakes and forgive others who have caused you emotional pain. And forgiveness stems from compassion. You cannot forgive until you develop a profound compassion for yourself and others, and understand that those who came into your life were put there for a reason—even if it was to teach you a painful lesson.

APPRECIATION

Learning to live in appreciation means not only going inside yourself to discover what is important to you, but also looking outside yourself to discover what will benefit others. When you live in appreciation, you can handle anything with compassion and grace, no matter what is going on around you.

Often when addicts and alcoholics are newly sober, they must deal with a backlog of shame and guilt. The shame can be from childhood abuse or neglect, lying, reckless conduct, or a direct result of self-destructive behaviors exhibited during addiction. According to the Law of Sobriety, focusing on appreciation for what is happening in the present helps them stop focusing on what they are ashamed of in their past.

Kristen's Story

Kristen was deeply entrenched in shame and guilt about how irresponsible her parenting had been during her drinking days. She had been drunk while driving her children to and from school and at most of their activities. She could not let go of the pain she had caused her family. Constantly thinking about the foolish chances she took driving her children while intoxicated pushed her deeper into shame, and she continued to relapse. This is a classic example of how what we manifest—the bad as well as the good—comes back to us.

During her recovery, Kristen started to become more active in her children's lives by volunteering at school and attending their school open houses. These activities made her feel good about her parenting efforts. Once she started to concentrate on the positive changes she was making in her relationship with her children, she was no longer tempted to relapse. When she stopped obsessing about her previous destructive behavior and instead focused on how present she had become for her children in her sobriety, she was able to move on and embrace her new, sober life with appreciation for all it offered her. By embracing the Law of Sobriety, she allowed a deep and profound compassion and forgiveness for herself to flow into her being. Her energy of forgiveness and compassion attracted more appreciation for the future she was creating. By walking through the pain of her past, she was able to transform herself and gain clarity about her purpose as a mother. The past no longer haunted Kristen, but instead became a life lesson. Her guilt decreased when she focused on appreciation and forgiveness rather than pain and regret. Her compassionate nature was awakened when she accessed the Law of Sobriety, giving her the courage to see hope in a situation that had previously seemed unbearable to her. She woke up each day with appreciation for the gifts sobriety had given her. She was able to let go of her shame from the past, accept her disease, and know she truly had a purpose: to be the best mother she could be for her children.

When you stop giving negative energy to your stories, you take back your personal power, allowing these stories to become lessons in forgiveness and compassion for yourself and others.

LEARNING TO FORGIVE

For most of us, forgiveness is extremely difficult. And, as hard as it is to forgive others, it's even harder to forgive ourselves. The Law of Sobriety says that your energy is strengthened when you let go of the judgments you have made about yourself because you are an addict or an alcoholic. There is nothing to gain by blaming and shaming who you are because you have a disease. This type of attitude gives rise to a victim mentality—"Nothing ever works out for me"—and it reduces your ability to attract positive events to your life. The past is who you were, not who you are now and who you are becoming.

Forgiving yourself enables you to create the positive energy that will bring positive outcomes into your life. Not forgiving yourself means living in constant pain and regret. When you hold on to your pain, it continues to cut you down. Instead, stop and examine your pain and all the beliefs that surround it; you will see there was a purpose for it, a lesson to be learned. On the other side of pain is perfection. Once you realize the purpose, the healing can begin. So many clients have told me that once they learned to forgive themselves and others, their lives were transformed forever.

> To forgive is the highest, most beautiful form of love. In return, you will receive untold peace and happiness.
>
> —Robert Mueller

It is important to remember that *you create your reality*. The situation you are in is a direct result of your belief system. I have had many clients who were not willing to see that the emotional pain in their lives was of their own making.

Patty's Story

A person with a history of unsuccessful relationships with men: that was how Patty described herself. She hooked up exclusively with men whom she felt she could control in some way. She tended to choose men who earned less money than she did, and believed this gave her the upper hand in these relationships. She believed they wouldn't leave her because they needed her. Having this type of control over the relationship gave her the illusion that she would never be abandoned—as she had been by her father. Patty's father had been physically abusive, and then left his family when she was only seven years old. In her early childhood, she had no sense of safety and security.

As a teenager, Patty developed an eating disorder in an effort to gain the control she had lost at a very young age. Psychologists believe that people often develop an eating disorder as a way to control a chaotic or dysfunctional environment. By controlling what they eat, they feel a sense of control that they do not have in other areas of their lives. Patty was treated for her eating disorder and was able to manage it. She got married soon after. It was a quick grab for the security and control she craved. The problem was she never gave herself the time to figure out who she really wanted to be and what she wanted to do with her life. Patty did not continue in a recovery program for her eating disorder, and her need for control never really went away. Although the eating disorder did not resurface, she still had not dealt with her underlying problems.

Patty immediately became pregnant. Her husband decided to go to graduate school, so Patty worked two jobs she despised to support her family. After her husband graduated and established himself in his new career, he abandoned her and their young child. Patty felt used and resentful when she thought about the many years she had supported him as he pursued his dream. She told anyone who would listen how awful her ex-husband was and how he had abandoned her just as her father had done. She also began drinking. She saw herself as a victim and had never worked through a true recovery plan for her eating disorder. Her drinking progressed and she got closer to crossing the line into alcoholism.

There is no question that her ex-husband and her father behaved reprehensibly. But what Patty could not see is that sometimes you attract people, places, and things in your life that mirror your past issues so that you can learn from them and heal. She expected her husband to abandon her, just as her father had, which is why she tried to keep him dependent on her. It was no accident that he left her life as fast as he had entered it; she got exactly what she expected. Rather than learning from this experience, it reaffirmed her belief that she must not be "good enough," and that if she couldn't keep the upper hand in a relationship, she would be abandoned again and again.

Holding fast to this belief, she re-created the trauma from her marriage over and over in her subsequent relationships by trying to make men dependent on her and then being abandoned by them. She felt deep resentment over these failed relationships, and this resentment caused her drinking to escalate even more. Patty became an alcoholic.

Our work together focused on helping her to see these situations in a different way. This new view enabled her to let go of all the resentment and fear that was keeping her stuck in a swirl of negative energy. She learned that although her ex-husband had hurt her deeply and her subsequent relationships further validated her "undesirability," they also became her greatest teachers. She was able to see that these relationships were a chance to heal her past wounds—a kind of "do over" until she was able to find the right path. By doing this work, her drinking decreased and eventually she found her way to sobriety. Following the Law of Sobriety helped her to forgive the men who had hurt her. She gained a deep compassion not only for herself, but for her ex-husband and all the other men she had felt had betrayed her.

I do not believe that sheer suffering teaches. If suffering alone taught, all the world would be wise, since everyone suffers. To suffering must be added mourning, understanding, patience, love, openness, and a willingness to remain vulnerable.

—Joseph Addison

By surrendering to this revelation, Patty also realized that what she despised in her ex-husband and the others was really just a projection of how she felt about herself—unlovable. She learned that unless you work through and resolve your past issues, you will attract individuals who personify the part of yourself that you despise. Her marriage and the other relationships reflected back to Patty everything she hated in herself. Patty's ex-husband and the others had abandoned her, but she had abandoned herself a very long time ago by believing there was nothing to love about herself. She expected to be abandoned, and she got exactly what she expected. Her failed relationships forced her to face the truth about herself—the truth she had been denying. It was much easier to blame them for all her pain, but it was pain she kept setting herself up for. Once Patty forgave these men, she was able to free up her energy and heal her original wound—her father's abandonment.

The Law of Sobriety works when you refocus your energy from judgment, blame, resentment, and rage to forgiveness, compassion, and the willingness to see every situation as purposefully perfect, just as it unfolds.

If you are now in a state of ill health, there is something, somebody, or some memory you need to forgive and release from your feelings forever. Perhaps you are not consciously aware of what it is. But your subconscious mind, which is the storehouse of your feelings, emotions, and memories, knows what it is. It will respond with release and healing when you give yourself treatments in forgiveness.

—From *The Dynamic Laws of Prosperity*
by Catherine Ponder

Tools for Change
Finding a Way to Forgive

It's not easy to forgive past hurts. But when you forgive someone, although you are sending the thoughts outward, the Law of Sobriety says this is also an internal process. It allows you to forgive yourself as you forgive others. This exercise will help you find a way to forgiveness.

- Begin to breathe in someone you have been feeling resentment toward and who you need to forgive.
- Write, "The person or situation I send forgiveness to is_____." (Examples might be, "I send forgiveness to my boss who fired me" or "I send forgiveness to my ex-boyfriend.")
- Write down the feelings that brought you pain about the person or situation you are forgiving. (Examples might be, "I felt betrayed and angry when my boss fired me" or "I felt scared and insecure when my ex-boyfriend verbally abused me.")
- Now breathe in and breathe out, letting go of the person or situation that caused you pain. Take a moment to feel compassion in your heart for whatever it was that caused you to suffer.
- Embrace the truth that whatever caused you pain was an experience brought to you for a purpose. Remind yourself that the universe always offers us the opportunity to heal through the process of forgiveness.

Scientific evidence reveals that the capacity to forgive yields both psychological and physical benefits. A 2004 study done by Dr. Joanna Maselko at the Harvard School of Public Health looked at how the capacity to forgive oneself and others affects a person's emotional well-being. It concluded that people who are more able to forgive are also more likely to report being very happy and less likely to report having psychological distress. Among married people, highly forgiving people were 1.5 times more likely to be very satisfied with their marriages than less forgiving people.

Dr. Frederic Luskin at Stanford University also studied forgiveness and relationships in a series of studies published in 2003 called the Stanford Forgiveness Project. The results showed that forgiveness offered "both emotional and physical benefits, from decreased feelings of hurt, depression, and stress, to increased feelings of optimism and willingness to forgive others." Forgiveness also makes room for vital energy that can be used for creative endeavors.

How far you go in life depends on your being tender with the young, compassionate with the aged, sympathetic with the striving and tolerant of the weak and strong. Because someday in life you will have been all of these.

—George Washington Carver

One of the tools we have already talked about is living "as if." In other words, you can act as if you already embody forgiveness, and the Law of Sobriety says the positive benefits of this forgiveness will manifest in your life. For example, if you are feeling uncomfortable with the newness of sobriety (which is often the case), visualize yourself one year from now embracing the peace and serenity that recovery is bringing you because you have forgiven yourself—even if you don't truly feel that way right now. Embracing the energy of tranquillity allows it to flow through your body easily and effortlessly, and it actually has a better chance of becoming a reality.

The ninth step of twelve-step programs asks you to make amends to the people you have harmed. The process of making amends gives you the opportunity to reveal yourself to others, thus freeing you from having to hide your true essence. It enables you to heal the past with others, and as you do, you learn how to forgive yourself. You begin to feel the joy that forgiveness and compassion for yourself and others brings. You move away from destroying your life with alcohol, drugs, and other destructive behaviors and awaken to the realization that you never again have to harm yourself or anyone else. This doesn't mean you relinquish responsibility for past transgressions, but instead, you are free to let go of past resentments of yourself and others so that you can heal. The *Alcoholics Anonymous Big Book* says resentment "destroys more alcoholics than anything." That's because if you cannot let go of past resentments, the only person who suffers is *you*; hurting others is really just hurting yourself all over again.

Our inventory enables us to settle with the past. When this is done, we are really able to leave it behind us. When our inventory is carefully taken, and we have made peace with ourselves, the conviction follows that tomorrow's challenges can be met as they come.

—From *Twelve Steps and Twelve Traditions*, Alcoholics Anonymous

Tools for Change
Visualizing Forgiveness

Some tools you can use to embrace forgiveness include telling your story to someone you trust, reframing your story with a new set of eyes, and viewing situations as being crucial to your growth rather than as a catastrophe. Here is a visualization exercise you can use to forgive yourself and others. Put aside ten to twenty minutes a day for this visualization.

• Find a comfortable position, close your eyes, and begin to breathe in through your nose and out through your mouth. Do this several times. Begin to imagine pictures of the past that bring up feelings of resentment. These can be people, places, or situations. Spend time observing yourself forgiving these people, places, or situations. Notice how these situations were brought to you for a reason and how you are shifting from a place of judgment to seeing the perfection of these experiences.

• Observe your body letting go of anger, resentment, hurt, sadness, fear, blame, and shame, and feel the lightness of releasing this negative energy. Know that you have grown from these lessons, no matter how painful.

• Visualize yourself in an empty space with clouds swirling around you. Know that you are the creator of your reality. Know that the sacred space you are in is one of healing and that this space is always available for you to access when you need to let go or release judgments of yourself and of others.

• Now, ask yourself the following questions to find out if you have forgiven yourself.

   ✓ Do I view this situation as a kind of healing and as an opportunity for growth in my recovery?

✓ Am I participating in this situation as a victim or am I able to see my part without judgment?

✓ Am I able to reframe my negative thoughts about this situation and see it as a gift of my sobriety?

✓ Do I accept my feelings as just feelings, or am I judging them harshly?

✓ Am I letting negative thoughts about my disease prevent me from accepting where I am right here and now?

✓ Do I still resent or fear someone whom I haven't been able to forgive?

✓ What am I gaining by not forgiving the people, places, and situations that hurt me?

Once you have answered these questions, create affirmation statements of forgiveness.

✓ I am aware that I attract people into my life to help me with my healing process.

✓ I release all the negative energies of judgment and resentment to positive energies of forgiveness for all the people, places, and situations in my life that have taught me lessons.

✓ My past mistakes have all led me toward my recovery process.

✓ I am grateful to all those people, places, and situations that mirror my imperfections so that I can learn and grow from them.

✓ I let go of defensiveness, grudges, revenge, and retaliation toward those I believe have harmed me and instead forgive them for their transgressions and forgive myself for any part I played in the situation.

✓ I am willing to see my past pain from a different perspective, which allows me to release any blocked energy that is still holding that emotional pain.

✓ By learning to forgive, I am no longer a victim of my circumstances.

EMBRACING COMPASSION

Through the process of forgiving, we give ourselves and others the gift of compassion. This is one of the most profound ways we can repair our past wounds. All the love we give to ourselves and to others is attracted back to us, according to the Law of Sobriety. The more compassionate we are, the more the universe responds with powerful, positive vibrations.

Psychologist Martin Seligman, director of the University of Pennsylvania's Positive Psychology Center, found that forgiveness and mercy, and the ability to give and receive love, were among the top twenty-four attributes (he calls them character strengths) associated with high levels of life satisfaction. (Others include optimism, curiosity, hope, and gratitude.)

Compassion is also a central concept of most religions and spiritual practices. Buddhists believe you cannot attain enlightenment without compassion, and they have many practices for cultivating compassion for oneself and all living beings. There is a Buddhist concept known as metta—a word that means loving-kindness—in which the heart opens unconditionally, encompassing everything with acceptance, awareness, and compassion. Metta is love in its purest form. It is an unconditional type of love and compassion that is drawn from an open heart, in which giving love itself is the gift. Cultivating metta helps overcome anger, resentment, and hurt and helps develop empathy, kindness, and appreciation. But you need not be a Buddhist to appreciate the idea and to sincerely wish for the well-being of others.

We are more alike, my friends, than we are unalike.
—From *Human Family* by Maya Angelou

Tools for Change
A Loving-Kindness Exercise

Spend a few minutes a day spreading loving-kindness in the universe. Breathe in love and breathe out compassion for yourself. Then breathe in compassion and breathe out love for all sentient beings. Repeat the following words.

- May I be secure.
- May I feel joy.
- May I have a sense of well-being and contentment.
- May I live in peace and serenity.

Embody those words within yourself. Then repeat the following words.

- May you be secure.
- May you feel joy.
- May you have a sense of well-being and contentment.
- May you live in peace and serenity.

Embrace those words and, in the most compassionate way, send those thoughts out to the entire universe. This is how the Law of Sobriety offers healing to everyone on the planet.

Ultimately, the reason why love and compassion bring the greatest happiness is simply that our nature cherishes them above all else. The need for love lies at the very foundation of human existence. It results from the profound interdependence we all share with one another.

—Tenzin Gyatso, the 14th Dalai Lama

One of the ways you can practice compassion is by acknowledging another person's perspective. This is a way of uniting compassion and wisdom. In the *Alcoholics Anonymous Big Book,* there's a discussion of how when we are thinking about people who have done us harm, compassion and wisdom can indeed unite. It says, "We realized that the people who wronged us were perhaps spiritually sick. Though we did not like their symptoms and the way they disturbed us, they, like ourselves were sick too. We asked God to help us show them the same tolerance, pity, and patience that we would cheerfully grant a sick friend."

FINDING A WAY TO FORGIVE THROUGH COMPASSION

I have heard many stories of forgiveness, but this is perhaps the one that has moved me the most. I thank Alida Schuyler, M.S., P.C.C., director of Crossroads Recovery Coaching, Inc., for sharing it with me.

Alida's Story

"I had about twelve years of recovery when I became deeply afraid that I would drink again. I was flunking out of medical school, watching a dream dissolve, and squirming with shame. I called a wise healer and told her that I was afraid I was going to drink again because I felt like a screwup and hated feeling that way again—especially in recovery. My friend instructed me to forgive everyone who made me feel like a screwup. I agreed to do that, even though I didn't know how. In my family there were no examples of forgiveness, so I had to figure out my own way to forgive.

"I realized quite quickly that feeling like a screwup was a feeling I'd had as long as I could remember. I decided it would be easier to forgive everyone, rather than try to figure out who should be forgiven. Here is how I did it.

"I started with my early childhood and moved forward through the years. For instance, I remembered that when I was in kindergarten, on a very cold morning, my brother told me to touch the mailbox with my tongue. I did, and my tongue stuck to the metal and I had to wait there for him to bring water to thaw my tongue off. It still made me mad. How could my brother do that to a little girl—to his own sister?

"It was clear that thinking over these incidents from my point of view was not going to bring about forgiveness. I understood then that I was going to have to try to see things from the point of view of the person who harmed me. I didn't want to do that alone, so I imagined that my higher power was sitting with me and that we would watch these 'movies' together—first my version, then the version of the other person. Afterward, my higher power and I would talk about what we saw. I imagined all this in my mind's eye.

"In the case of my brother, I learned when I saw the 'movie' from his point of view that he had tried licking the mailbox himself on a morning that wasn't so cold. The tip of his tongue stuck a little bit but it came off quite easily when he warmed the mailbox with his breath. My brother thought I would have the same experience and was surprised when my tongue froze and I couldn't remove it. He was embarrassed when he went for the warm water and my mother asked him, 'How could you be so stupid?'

"It was easy to forgive my brother when I saw it from his point of view. Yes, I would have liked him to say he was sorry, but he was a kid who had just been chewed out by his mother. My higher power and I both forgave him and we moved on to the next childhood 'movie.'

"I did the same thing with painful memories about my sister. I showed my higher power my version, and then we watched again from my sister's point of view. When I looked at things from her point of view, I could see why she was jealous and mean. I was funny and silly and made my parents laugh. My sister wanted to get the same easy affection from them but couldn't. I was able to have compassion when I saw things from my sister's point of view.

"I went through many incidents in my early childhood, watching, understanding, and forgiving. I saw that I really was okay in spite of how I felt at the time.

"The challenge came when the incidents involved incest, pedophilia, physical violence, and similar events. In some cases I became angry with my higher power: 'How could you have let these things happen to me?' I was so mad. It was extremely painful to watch the movies of these incidents, but I did. I remember one of being abused by an older boy. I was surprised by how young and pretty I was. The boy was five years older than me, but now, as an adult, I would consider him a kid too. I could handle that person. I couldn't all those years ago, but I definitely could now.

"I remember my higher power asking me if I was willing to see the other person's movie. I didn't want to, but I remembered why I was doing this—so I wouldn't drink again. I agreed to see the movie.

"When I saw it from the boy's point of view, I saw how insecure he was. He had his first high school girlfriend but knew nothing about female bodies and was using me to learn. I saw that he was selfish but also ignorant of how harmful his actions would be to me. I was able to forgive him because as I watching things from his point of view, he changed from being a huge ogre to being a stupid teenage kid, and I recognized that I was more powerful than him. I could see how afraid he was of not knowing about girls. Yes, he was immensely selfish and ignorant. But I was strong, healthy, and capable of forgiving him if I chose to. I did forgive him, and it set me free.

"It took days and days to go through this process. I got through my life, all the way through high school. It freed up immense amounts of energy. I no longer wanted to drink."

Finally, we begin to see that all people, including ourselves, are to some extent emotionally ill as well as frequently wrong, and then we approach true tolerance and see what real love for our fellows actually means. It will become more and more evident as we go forward that it is pointless to become angry, or to get hurt by people who, like us, are suffering from the pains of growing up.

—From *Twelve Steps and Twelve Traditions,* Alcoholics Anonymous

---

The fellowship of a twelve-step program is another way to develop a deeper compassion for others. Just knowing that you are not alone and that others, too, suffer from the disease of substance abuse can be profoundly therapeutic and healing. Many clients have told me that when they enter a twelve-step meeting, they suddenly feel they are "home." They can relate to others on a level never before achieved in their relationships. There is a profound love and compassion for their fellow members that goes beyond anything they have ever known. The Law of Sobriety is at work when it draws like-minded people together in a room for healing and hope.

I have seen the same compassion in recovery psychotherapy groups. There is an overwhelming sense of being a part of something much greater than themselves for all participants. Call it a higher power, the universe, a life force, or the Law of Sobriety—something changes for these group members that brings a sense of compassion for others that was not there before. These individuals reflect back to one another who they truly are, and that is the Law of Sobriety in action. They take off their masks and false identities and relate to one another in a nonjudgmental way. By validating one another's very core, they move together toward love and compassion.

Being acknowledged for who you are is one of the greatest and most compassionate gifts you can give or receive. When there is no judgment, there is love. Even if you aren't completely ready to accept another, start wherever you are.

Carol's and Brie's Stories

At one of my therapy groups, Carol talked about the fact that she was physically abused as a child. She became quite emotional while telling the story of how she suffered years of torment by her father, and how angry she was with her mother for not protecting Carol and her siblings. While listening to this story, Brie, another member of the group, remembered how her husband had physically abused her and her children, too. Suddenly, Brie felt overwhelmed by guilt and shame—feelings she had not acknowledged for a long time—because she had not protected her own children. But Brie also had deep compassion for Carol for being willing to share her story so honestly.

Brie went home that evening and had nightmares for the next few days. When the group met the following week, she told us how guilty she felt for not protecting her own children. Brie was afraid Carol would judge her for not protecting her kids, just as Carol's own mother had not protected her. But instead, Carol felt the same compassion for Brie that Brie had felt for Carol the week before.

The experience was transformative for both Brie and Carol. They had both abused alcohol and drugs for a very long time; each woman had been trying to erase the emotional scars endured in physically abusive relationships. When their stories were shared and they felt validated and accepted, each was able to move toward compassion for themselves and for each other, releasing negative energy that had been blocked up inside of them for years.

When you embrace your pain rather than hide from it, it often diminishes or even disappears. This is an example of how accepting your pain and giving yourself permission to know it paves the way for you to let the pain go. When you do, the Law of Sobriety can help you transform it into love and compassion.

Tools for Change
Meditating for Compassion

One of the ways to access your compassion is to engage in a karuna meditation. Karuna means compassion. Buddhists believe karuna is essential to enlightenment, and many branches of Buddhism have specific ways of meditating to cultivate compassion. Karuna is especially important to Tibetan Buddhists. They believe one path to enlightenment is by cultivating the qualities of love, compassion, generosity, and patience. In fact, a study done in 2008 at the University of Wisconsin-Madison on Tibetan monks found that positive emotions such as lovingkindness and compassion can be learned. MRI scans of the monks's brains revealed that brain circuits used to detect emotions and feelings were dramatically changed in monks who had extensive experience practicing compassion meditation.

In *The Way of the Bodhisattva*, the eighth-century Indian master Shantideva says, "Strive at first to meditate upon the sameness of yourself and others. In joy and sorrow all are equal; thus be guardian of all, as of yourself."

• Get comfortable, close your eyes, and allow your mouth to drop into a half smile. Resonate feelings of joy and peace in your heart.

Begin by allowing yourself to receive loving acceptance of yourself and let go of any feelings you might have of being unworthy or less than.

- Carry that loving-kindness to someone, such as a sponsor, psychotherapist, spiritual advisor, or someone else you deeply trust. Then continue to transfer that loving-kindness to those close to you, such as your family and friends.

- Continue to spread that loving-kindness to someone neutral, perhaps someone you see at the market or at a twelve-step meeting but have not had the chance to talk to. Then continue spreading feelings of loving-kindness to someone you resent or who you feel has caused you pain.

- Continue to send out these loving vibrations to all beings and then out to the whole planet, and finally the entire universe.

Rather than repeating affirmations, you can use the karuna practice to set intentions of loving-kindness and compassion toward those you focused on earlier, such as family, friends, the planet, and the universe. For example:

✓ I am aware of my own suffering.
✓ I am aware of the suffering of others.
✓ I am aware that all suffering is the same.
✓ I feel compassion for myself.
✓ I feel compassion for all who suffer.
✓ I feel compassion for all.

APPRECIATION AND GRATITUDE

The Law of Sobriety says you should begin appreciating your sobriety even if you haven't achieved it yet. If you are on the road to sobriety, believe you have already manifested the joy and peace it is bringing you. Thank the universe for giving you the blessings you have received because of your recovery. By doing this, you move yourself closer to taking the action steps necessary to achieve sobriety or to maintain the sobriety you already have. Breathe in the gifts of sobriety, such as improved relationships, clarity, focus, happiness, and living in truth and appreciation. The more you express appreciation for what you already have, the better chance you have of receiving more of the same blessings.

When our hearts are God-centered and filled with love and laughter, we'll find no experience too difficult to handle. No problem will evade its solution for long. An attitude of love promises us gratitude in abundance. We'll never doubt that all is well when love is at our center.

—From *Worthy of Love* by Karen Casey

The Law of Sobriety encourages you to cultivate an attitude of gratitude and appreciation, rather than one of judgment, disapproval, and criticism. Gratitude enables you to stay in the present, looking at all the things in your life you are grateful for. So often alcoholics and addicts are either thinking about the past or worrying about the future. This causes them to live with endless anxiety. By appreciating what is happening at this very moment, you are released from that fearfulness and insecurity. Gratitude allows you to stop comparing yourself with others, thus diminishing feelings such as jealousy and envy.

Substance abusers often exhibit the "more" disease, where enough is never enough. That's how it is with drugs and alcohol, and the same holds true with material things. They often want fancier cars, bigger houses, a better body, more money in the bank, a better relationship, a better job, and the list goes on. Once alcohol and drugs are removed, they continue to look for more and more things to fill that void. These external things are nice for a short while, but when the newest thing is no longer satisfying, cravings increase for the imagined "whatever" that is lacking. Substance abusers are unable to be satisfied with what is, and the need just grows—similar to the way the need for drugs and alcohol grows as tolerance develops. Material things become just another addiction.

When you take your first steps toward recovery, you also need to sit back and notice what you already have in your life. By doing this, you release the negative energy it takes to keep striving for more and more of what you think you need to be happy and fulfilled. If what you have matches your values, then you truly do have everything you could possibly need or desire. If you are living your true nature and are out of the denial you embraced when you were using, then you have a lot to appreciate and a lot to be grateful for.

When I picked my first sponsor at an AA meeting, I remember the members telling me to choose someone who had "what you want." At the time I thought they meant material possessions, not spiritual attributes. I picked a sponsor who had a good-looking and successful husband, a big house, a nice car, a career in entertainment, and all the material things I so desperately wanted and thought would fulfill me. But as time went on, I learned that what I really needed was a sponsor who had what I wanted *on the inside*. I had a spiritual emptiness, or what the twelve-step community might call a "soul sickness," that needed to be filled up. Picking a sponsor who had all the goodies on the outside wasn't going to help me fill that inner void. What I needed was a higher power and a sponsor who was spiritually fit to lead me there. I later found the sponsor who resonated exactly what I needed at the time. She helped me find my way through my sobriety with a sense of grace and serenity that no external thing could ever provide for me.

What is so wonderful about gratitude and the Law of Sobriety is that when you focus on what you truly appreciate, the universe just brings you more to appreciate. Unfortunately, if you focus on what you are missing, the universe responds by giving you an even greater sense that you're missing out. You cannot be appreciative and negative at the same time. If you are having a difficult day or find yourself depressed, turn your emotions around by focusing on something you appreciate. Maybe it is your pet, or something simple like your cuddly blanket or the rose bush outside that is blooming. Having a strong focus on appreciation enables you to get in touch with your inner core. And then fear, regret, judgment, resentment, and blame can be released.

Tools for Change
Cultivating Gratitude

There are many ways to remind yourself to be grateful for what you have in your life. Try these gratitude exercises.

- Start your day or close your day with a list of things, people, and experiences for which you are grateful. Express this as a prayer or blessing.
- Keep a Gratitude Journal listing all the things for which you are grateful.
- Tell each individual who helps you or gives you service in some way, not just "thank you" but how grateful you are.
- Help any children you know to understand the importance of gratitude and to practice it.

- Write notes of gratitude to people—especially when they don't expect it.
- Always arrive with a gift of gratitude when someone has invited you to their home or to some event. If you cannot afford to buy a gift, make one!
- Bring tokens of gratitude to your coworkers at least once a month.
- Send birthday cards to people you care about with expressions of how grateful you are to have them in your life. This can be by mail or by e-mail.
- Share your gratitude not just with those to whom you are grateful, but with others who know them, so that the recipient knows that you are proud to sing his or her praises.
- Go on a Gratitude Journey: take a walk, a bike ride, or a cross-country ski in the outdoors and just allow your heart to express your gratitude for the beauty you see and all things in your life.
- Do a Gratitude Survey: survey your amazing body and mind and offer gratitude for each and every part. Don't forget your smile!
- Be thankful for the universe itself! Without this great force of energy and spirit, you would not exist today as the grateful being you are.

This exercise was written by and is used with permission from Jackie Lapin, author of The Art of Conscious Creation: How You Can Transform the World, *who guides you on how to consciously create your life and become a better, faster manifestor. For books, tools, and daily manifesting tips, go to www.theartofconsciouscreation.com.*

I am married to one of the most grateful people I know. There is not a day that goes by that he doesn't appreciate everything he has. Even after two shoulder surgeries in the past year, which have left him with occasional physical pain, he wakes up with a positive outlook on life. His positive energy is certainly contagious. Our marriage is an example of the Law of Sobriety at work. He was once homeless, having lost every material thing he possessed; but he never lost hope that things could turn around—and they did. He got back into the industry he had left when he was using, was reunited with his family, met me (which was a miracle for both of us), and built a life again.

Jack's Story

Not everyone is as lucky as I am to have a spouse who lives life in appreciation. I have witnessed couples in recovery who can't seem to get enough appreciation from one another. Jack always felt his wife should know what he needed without being told—he expected her to be a mind reader. He was constantly disappointed when she didn't anticipate his needs or meet his expectations. One time Jack was sick with the flu and felt his wife should "just know" how to take care of him. She didn't bring soup home for him after work, and he felt that because she didn't bring it, she must not care about him or the fact that he was sick. Jack never told her how he was feeling, but he ignored her the entire night. When I asked him how his wife was supposed to know he wanted soup when he hadn't said anything, his response was, "That is what a good wife would do."

In this situation, Jack was unable to appreciate—or even notice—the things his wife did for him that expressed her care and concern. He focused exclusively on what he felt he was *not* getting and did not appreciate anything he *was* getting. After some work in therapy, Jack came to realize that he had unmet needs from his childhood that he projected onto his wife. He realized this was also a problem in other aspects of his life. He needed constant validation and acknowledgment from others, and when he didn't get it, he felt angry, hurt, helpless, and sometimes hopeless. He was depending on others to validate him, and that meant he was constantly disappointed and angry.

Whatever you think people are withholding from you—praise, appreciation, assistance, loving care, and so on—give it to them. You don't have it? Just act as if you had it, and it will come. Then, soon after you start giving, you will start receiving. You cannot receive what you don't give.

—From *A New Earth*
by Eckhart Tolle

Once Jack realized those unmet needs from the past were at the root of his issues, he was able to let go of his need for constant appreciation from others. And with that clarity, he began to have more compassion for himself. He also learned that when he needed something from his wife, he had to tell her rather than holding it in and becoming resentful or hostile toward her. These new revelations changed their relationship. They went from being critical of each other to compassionate, from being insensitive to each other's needs to an increased intimacy, and from resenting each other to rejoicing in their newfound love and respect for each other.

It is imperative that you have deep appreciation for *who you are,* not for what you do. The more you appreciate yourself, the better your chance of getting where you want to go and becoming who you want to be. At the beginning of this chapter I said that when you live in appreciation, you can handle anything with compassion and grace, no matter what is going on around you. It is vital to take a few moments at some point each day to make a list of the things you are grateful for. You can write down your list or just go through it in your mind. Allowing yourself to appreciate the small wonders around you wakes up that part of you that longs to forgive and have compassion for yourself. How often do you have profound compassion for those around you but no compassion for yourself? Take the time now to forgive yourself. Aren't you doing the best you can in your recovery? Remind yourself of that. Then breathe in appreciation for all your progress and breathe out the compassion and forgiveness you deserve.

Tools for Change
Meditating on What Is Around You

A gratitude mediation will help you focus on what is around you and develop a new appreciation for it.

- Take a few moments to begin breathing deeply. Breathe in through your nose and out through your mouth. Take a few more breaths.
- Thoughts of what you have or don't have may come up as you practice this gratitude meditation. Just notice the thoughts that come and go. Don't judge them or follow them.
- Begin to focus on something you are thankful for. It could be as simple as the fact that you are still breathing.
- Take a moment to notice what is good in your life. Don't get caught up in the feeling that you should be grateful about anything in particular. Just be curious; if something comes up that you do appreciate, be open to it. Give yourself permission to not feel guilty if a feeling of gratitude doesn't arise. Let that be okay. Let gratitude come up naturally and effortlessly.
- Notice how appreciation feels in your body, where your energy is flowing smoothly or is blocked. Allow whatever comes up to spread throughout your body. Notice what brings you contentment and ease.
- Now take a moment to consciously think about a person, place, or situation you appreciate. Ask yourself the following questions:
  ✓ Who and what do I appreciate at this very moment?

✓ What has my sobriety given me?

✓ Who can I thank for supporting me during my recovery?

✓ Who can I show gratitude to?

✓ Why am I thankful for the many blessings in my life?

✓ How can I remove the blocks that keep me from being grateful?

Once you have answered these questions, allow yourself to embody the following affirmations.

✓ I am grateful to be sober.

✓ I am grateful for the newfound energy sobriety has given me.

✓ I value my sobriety and myself as I continue on the road of recovery.

✓ I project an attitude of gratitude.

✓ I choose to focus on appreciation.

✓ I feel appreciated today.

✓ I appreciate the lessons I am learning during my journey through recovery.

READER/CUSTOMER CARE SURVEY

We care about your opinions! Please take a moment to fill out our online Reader Survey at **http://survey.hcibooks.com.**
As a **"THANK YOU"** you will receive a **VALUABLE INSTANT COUPON** towards future book purchases
as well as a **SPECIAL GIFT** available only online! Or, you may mail this card back to us.

(PLEASE PRINT IN ALL CAPS)

First Name _____ MI. _____ Last Name _____

Address _____ City _____

State _____ Zip _____ Email _____

1. Gender
☐ Female ☐ Male

2. Age
☐ 8 or younger
☐ 9-12 ☐ 13-16
☐ 17-20 ☐ 21-30
☐ 31+

3. Did you receive this book as a gift?
☐ Yes ☐ No

4. Annual Household Income
☐ under $25,000
☐ $25,000 - $34,999
☐ $35,000 - $49,999
☐ $50,000 - $74,999
☐ over $75,000

5. What are the ages of the children living in your house?
☐ 0 - 14 ☐ 15+

6. Marital Status
☐ Single
☐ Married
☐ Divorced
☐ Widowed

7. How did you find out about the book?
(please choose one)
☐ Recommendation
☐ Store Display
☐ Online
☐ Catalog/Mailing
☐ Interview/Review

8. Where do you usually buy books?
(please choose one)
☐ Bookstore
☐ Online
☐ Book Club/Mail Order
☐ Price Club (Sam's Club, Costco's, etc.)
☐ Retail Store (Target, Wal-Mart, etc.)

9. What subject do you enjoy reading about the most?
(please choose one)
☐ Parenting/Family
☐ Relationships
☐ Recovery/Addictions
☐ Health/Nutrition
☐ Christianity
☐ Spirituality/Inspiration
☐ Business Self-help
☐ Women's Issues
☐ Sports

10. What attracts you most to a book?
(please choose one)
☐ Title
☐ Cover Design
☐ Author
☐ Content

TAPE IN MIDDLE; DO NOT STAPLE

Health Communications, Inc.
3201 SW 15th Street
Deerfield Beach FL 33442-9875

FOLD HERE

Comments

SIX

Living a Life of Right Action

Today, we can risk moving forward and trust
ourselves, with the guidance of our Higher Power,
to move in a right and orderly direction.

—From *Our Best Days*
by Sally Coleman and Nancy Hull-Mast

Living a life of right action means acting in accordance with who you are truly meant to be—not just doing what is right, but doing what is right *for you*. It means directing your energies toward what makes your heart sing. To live a life of right action, it is imperative to ask yourself whether the choices you are making align with your goals or with someone else's.

Addicts and alcoholics are often suffering from low self-esteem. It's important to realize that until you raise your sense of self-worth, you will continue to attract negative results into your life. Remember, the Law of Sobriety says you get what you expect to get. It is therefore vital to exercise your muscle of self-respect; when you respect yourself and the path you are on, you expect a better life—and you get it!

You build your self-respect by following the path that is yours and yours alone.

YOU NEED A PLAN

When you honor yourself, you know deep inside that your choices will bring true value to your life. You accomplish this by making conscious choices about your actions, rather than acting mindlessly or on impulse. Making conscious choices means bringing your direct awareness to all your actions. You think about your choices and where they will lead you, then decide what action is right for you. It is a work in progress in which you continually ask yourself, "What are my conscious actions creating for me?" If the choices you make do not resonate personal dignity and self-respect, then you have stepped out of a life of right action.

Tanya's Story

Tanya had been sober for a short time and was trying to decide whether or not she wanted to go back to school. It was important for her to analyze the positives and negatives associated with this choice. We discussed how courageous it was to tackle a return to school. She told me she was easily overwhelmed and knew her anxiety would resurface if she became too stressed. To add more pressure to her decision, her brother had graduated college with full honors in four years. She wasn't sure she could complete her studies at the same pace as her brother had completed his.

I suggested she come up with a step-by-step action plan that would meet her unique needs in her new sobriety. Although Tanya had fears about going to school, she decided to do it anyway, without letting her feelings run the show. After further thought, she decided to go back to school full time and follow her brother's path. She acted "as if" she had the confidence to return to school. This in itself was a positive step.

However, Tanya had not carefully formulated an action plan that was right for her in her particular situation. She kept her part-time job and signed up for more credits than she could handle. The time spent at work, in class, and studying prevented her from having a solid recovery plan of going to meetings, seeing her psychotherapist, and following through with other recovery goals she had set for herself. Unfortunately, six months after she'd started classes she was back in rehab, dealing with her addiction to antianxiety medicine plus a new problem—panic attacks.

Tanya sacrificed her own path to follow someone else's journey—in this case, her brother's. Her profound desire to please her parents and her brother pulled her off course, away from what was right for her. By not living a life of right action, she not only became over-stressed and suffered a relapse, but her self-esteem plummeted as well. Instead of making her family happy, she disappointed them even more. Tanya made an impulsive choice to start something without carefully thinking it through and setting out a plan for how she could best meet her academic goals without becoming overwhelmed.

When you decide to move forward in any endeavor, honoring who you are is extremely important. The best way to achieve that is to make a careful, detailed plan, laying out the steps of right action thoughtfully and carefully so you can reach your desired goal. Each step along the path is just as important as the final goal you set for yourself, and you cannot cut corners. Getting where you want to be by a route that does not honor who you truly are is not living a life of right action. The Law of Sobriety says when you stray from your path, you will never get where you want to be.

To avoid stumbling along the way, your action plan should be broken up into bite-size pieces. Taking things slowly and methodically leaves you room to be open to making changes if your plan needs revision or if you realize you are taking on more than you can handle. Addicts and alcoholics sometimes engage in all-or-nothing thinking. In other words, if one thing doesn't go well or go their way, they often quit in midstream. After just one mistake, they may become judgmental and critical of themselves or blame others, and this keeps them from reaching their goals. People in twelve-step programs are often reminded not to quit "before the miracle happens." In other words, just because you have made a mistake or even relapsed, don't walk away and think you can't do it. *You can.* Thoughtful planning will give you a better chance of experiencing that miracle or reaching that goal.

The Law of Sobriety teaches you to plan things mindfully, with clarity and awareness, so you have a chance to reach your fullest potential. You learn to let go of the fears that have held you back and instead to trust your own innate wisdom to make the right choices in your life. You'll need a plan for living a life of right action, and that plan begins with setting goals. The process of goal setting will help you see where you want to go, and will also give you an action plan for getting there. The exercise on page 140 will help you identify and define your goals.

Until one is committed, there is hesitancy, the chance to draw back, always ineffectiveness. Concerning all acts of initiative (and creation), there is one elementary truth the ignorance of which kills countless ideas and splendid plans: that the moment one definitely commits oneself, the providence moves too. A whole stream of events issues from the decision, raising in one's favor all manner of unforeseen incidents, meetings and material assistance, which no man could have dreamt would have come his way.
—From *The Scottish Himalayan Expedition* by W.H. Murray

If you have trouble developing your action plan, you may need assistance. That's perfectly okay. Planning is a skill, and, like any skill, it must be learned. Perhaps you need a life coach, recovery coach, psychotherapist, sponsor, mentor, or spiritual advisor to help you figure out the steps in your plan and keep you accountable so you can reach your desired goals. There are always others willing to support you in a way that doesn't undermine your success. Not only is support available for the asking, but you also have a higher power, the universe, God, or whoever or whatever you believe in to help you move toward a life of right action. By believing that there is something greater than yourself, you can allow the wisdom of that higher power to guide you.

If you encounter resistance while setting your goals, know that this is perfectly normal. Resistance is when those old messages that no longer serve you (and, frankly, never did) come back to haunt you. It is that sabotaging voice that tells you, "Don't bother, you'll never succeed," "Give it up, you don't have what it takes," or "You aren't smart enough." Resistance is the sum total of every fear you have ever had. Fear does not believe you can succeed. Neither does fear's partner in crime, low self-worth. When you are feeling a lack of self-respect, resistance is most likely right around the corner. Just work through the resistance, acknowledge the feelings you are experiencing, let them go, and get back to setting your goals.

When you devote yourself to achieving your goal, you will not be bothered by shallow criticism. Nothing important can be accomplished if you allow yourself to be swayed by some trifling matter, always looking over your shoulder and wondering what others are saying or thinking. The key to achievement is to move forward along your chosen path with firm determination.

—From *Determination* by Daisaku Ikeda

Tools for Change
Set Your Goals

Living a life of right action begins with setting goals. Remember, goals can be flexible and can always be redefined if they no longer resonate with who you are becoming. Goals are there to move you forward—from the smallest of tasks to supporting your true life purpose.

Begin defining your goals by listing several categories of your life and what you would like to achieve within those categories. The purpose of this list is to gain clarity about what you would like to achieve in each of these areas. The categories may include:

- Intimate relationships
- Work/career
- Recovery
- Personal growth
- Physical surroundings
- Family and friends
- Fun and leisure
- Health and well-being
- Lifestyle/financial

For each category, set goals that you truly want—not what you think you "should" want. Set goals that are reasonable and that you know you have an excellent chance of achieving. For smaller tasks, set the goals one week or one month at a time. For example, in health and well-being, your goals might be to eat fruits and vegetables every day for a week or to exercise three times a week for a month.

For your long-term goals, think big from your heart, not from your ego. Don't obsess about how you are going to get there. Remember, the Law of Sobriety says that when you put out positive energy to the universe, with clarity and the conviction of your goals, it always responds. Positive energy comes from positive thoughts, and positive thoughts lead to the manifestation of your goals.

Some examples of goals might be:

- Intimate relationships: I will nurture the relationship I have
  with my soul mate.
- Work/career: I will feel energized by my job.
- Recovery: I will attend twelve-step meetings three times a week.
- Personal growth: I will attend workshops or read books that
  inspire me.
- Physical surroundings: I will organize my house so that I can free
  up energy to pursue other endeavors.
- Family and friends: I will spend time with people who are positive
  and believe in my recovery.
- Fun and leisure: I will spend more time hiking in the places I love.
- Health and well-being: I will spend twenty minutes a day
  meditating to reduce stress and to keep me in balance.
- Lifestyle/financial: I will spend time each week planning
  for my financial future.

Here are some general guidelines as you go through the process of
setting goals:

- Make a list of what benefits you will receive by accomplishing
  these goals or tasks.
- Reach out to others to gain support, resources, and wisdom
  on how to attain your goals.
- Be compassionate with yourself if you have not achieved a goal.
  Look at the situation without criticism or judgment of yourself.
  Figure out if the goal is still pertinent to your life purpose or
  your sobriety.
- Remain focused intently on your goals.
- Keep in mind that material success is never fulfilling by itself. Real

joy comes from having goals that also meet your physical, mental, and spiritual needs.

- Always keep an attitude of gratitude as you go through this process.
- Honor yourself when you do achieve a goal.
- Remember you always have a choice to change your mind if your goals no longer fit you.
- If you become overwhelmed by this exercise, slow down, breathe, and take each category one small step at a time.

KEEPING YOUR PROMISES

Another concept often presented in twelve-step programs is being "open and willing," and that includes being willing to take action. But it doesn't mean jumping into things impulsively. Addicts and alcoholics are famous for impulsive, impetuous acts—scoring drugs in dangerous neighborhoods or hunting down bars that are open at all hours of the night are all-too-familiar examples. Sobriety is the time for making well-thought-out, conscious choices.

You know when your actions are impulsive. You will be obsessed and driven, and all your energy will be focused on jumping into that activity. Sound familiar? Before making a decision, ask yourself, "Will this decision benefit everyone concerned? Does it align with my personal integrity?" Making decisions with integrity is a big part of acting in a way that is aligned with your values, standards, and truthfulness. It is about honoring yourself and others and doing what you say you are going to do.

The only thing that you believed in during your using days was your addiction. You could never count on yourself or anyone else who touched your life when you were abusing substances. In your addiction, you might have made many unkept promises and hurt many people. When you make decisions or promises that you cannot keep, the guilt of disappointing yourself or others can be paralyzing.

When you are sober, you are trustworthy. Others can trust you, and you can trust yourself. But you have to learn this truth. It is imperative to slow down before you act hastily in your recovery. Otherwise, you may start second-guessing whether you should have started something in the first place; you may decide to not follow through. Allow yourself the compassion to make decisions and set goals that are realistic, so you don't set yourself up to fail even before you have started. You have beaten yourself up enough about breaking promises during your using days.

However, don't make promises that are too simple, either. In sobriety, make promises you know you can keep by exerting the effort you know you can make. The trust will come.

We must become willing to take action—continuous action— to become who we can become. It takes awareness to become entirely ready. Slow down, stop doing, and be. Feel it.

—From *Drop the Rock: Removing Character Defects*
by Bill P., Todd W., and Sara S.

A promise can never be right or wrong; it is there to keep you on your path. Make promises that are clear, concise, and observable, so you have a better chance of keeping them. A promise you make to a family member might be, "I will be on time when I pick my kids up from school." You might make a promise to yourself to support your career aspirations, such as, "I promise to send out two résumés a day." A promise in sobriety might be, "I will always call someone when I feel like taking a drink or calling the drug dealer." Twelve-step programs always encourage newcomers to commit to doing a specific task at a meeting, such as being a greeter or making the coffee. These simple promises teach you how to show up and get things done. Self-esteem comes from keeping those promises and experiencing the satisfaction you and others will feel when you do. As your sense of worth grows, your promises can grow as well to embrace larger, long-term goals.

Promises give energy to your life purpose. Your words set the stage for your future visions to be realized. When your actions align with your promises, the intentions you put out to the universe become actualized. Suddenly, solutions show up. When the fog has lifted and you embrace the Law of Sobriety, you become more aware and can finally listen to what the universe has been trying to tell you. In twelve-step programs they say, "More will be revealed"—it means people and circumstances will show up at exactly the right time and in exactly the right place.

I will never forget the time I was at an AA meeting just before I was scheduled to take a trip to Hawaii. Because of the people I was traveling with, I knew there would be a lot of alcohol present. When the leader of the AA meeting asked if there were any individuals from out of town, one woman raised her hand and said she was from Hawaii. During the break I went up to that person and asked where I might find some twelve-step meetings near my hotel. Imagine my surprise when she said she worked next door to the hotel and would be happy to take me to a meeting. My simple action of going up to that person and reaching out brought me the blessing of meeting someone who could support my sobriety while I was out of town. When I went to Hawaii, she kept her promise to me. And I kept my promise to myself to attend meetings and stay sober. It was one of many coincidences I and others have experienced when we trusted the universe to support our sobriety.

On the other end of the spectrum, don't set yourself up for disappointment by believing in people who don't keep their word. You keep your promises to yourself; expect nothing less from others. Move on and let go of the resentments you have been harboring for those who have disappointed you by breaking their promises. Your path—the path of sobriety—leads you in another direction.

SHAPING YOUR OWN DESTINY

The Law of Sobriety says your right action brings right action back to you. It will not always happen on your schedule, but when you do the right thing, the universe eventually responds. The energy you put into your positive actions comes back around in positive ways. As we have seen, the reverse is also true: if your actions are destructive, that, too, will be returned to you. The decisions you make in your sobriety determine your destiny.

Have you ever sat in a twelve-step meeting and listened to how others have turned their lives around? That is the energetic force of right action at work. One of the greatest miracles I have witnessed was just such a situation.

Mona's Story

Mona was addicted to crack for a long time while raising her young children. She also suffered from deep depression and anxiety. Social services got involved and her children were taken from her due to her irresponsibility and neglect. The children were in the foster care system for a period of time; there were also times when they lived with their grandparents and times they spent with their biological fathers. Mona had children from two relationships and often the children were split up. It was a heartbreaking story.

But the ending was heartwarming. She finally went to a treatment facility that dealt with both her addictions and her mental illness.

After treatment, Mona moved into a sober living house and started to have supervised visits with her children. Because of her prior neglect, the courts did not approve of her spending time alone with them at first. As time went on, though, Mona earned the right to have her children every other weekend, and eventually had them 50 percent of the time (the rest of the time was shared with the children's fathers and grandparents).

She was so full of joy and peace when her children were finally able to return home—their home. She had been sober for quite a while by the time I met her, and has since become a chemical dependency counselor helping others who are recovering from their disease. Mona especially enjoys working with single parents who have gone through what she went through. She is a reminder for those still struggling with sobriety that there is always hope if you make choices that are based on right action.

The journey may not be easy and the payoff may not be immediate, but the empowerment you get from making good decisions is immeasurable. When you make the right choices, you have the opportunity to live in goodness and appreciation rather than dishonesty and desperation.

Our most defining moments come when we shift our energy toward right action rather than making decisions haphazardly or mindlessly. Understanding what the consequences may be when making certain decisions can be an effective way to gauge whether or not to move forward. And don't be afraid to make mistakes. Sometimes mistakes can be our greatest teachers. Knowing when a mistake was made and where you went wrong is a gift. It can lead you to figure out what right action you need to take to improve a situation or a relationship. Taking responsibility for the choices you have made means the results of a situation are yours. There is no one to blame when you become the creator of your own decisions.

> If you make a conscious, active choice and are willing to be held accountable for your behavior, you will feel much better about yourself, regardless of the choice you make.
>
> —From *Adult Children of Alcoholics*
> by Janet Geringer Woititz, Ed.D.

Take a moment to ask yourself what behaviors you engage in or actions you take that come from your highest virtues and standards. They can even be little decisions. For example, do you bring your own bags to the market instead of taking plastic bags, which can be harmful to the environment? Do you offer the last piece of bread to others at your table before grabbing it for yourself? These things may seem trivial, but try doing something similar and you will see how good you feel when you embrace the virtue of kindness. Do you offer your phone number to someone at a twelve-step meeting so he or she can call you if tempted to pick up a drink or use? Although this, too, can seem like a small gesture, you might end up saving someone's life. Be sure to think about the bigger issues, too. Do you judge others by what they have or don't have? Are you flexible or controlling in your relationships? Are you kind or abrasive when speaking to others? Do you live in a state of peacefulness or hostility?

Take the time to sift through your answers. Do they resonate with who you are or who you are becoming? Are they decisions that come from your authentic self or a false self? Do they resonate with right action?

It is time to evolve. But evolution can be slow. Remind yourself that change takes time and is a process. As the twelve-step programs suggest, "progress, not perfection" is the goal of living a life of right action.

DOING AND BEING

Another important principal of right action is balancing your actions between doing and being. Doing involves performing actions and creating methods for achieving things in the material world. For example, doing might concern how good your grades are in school, how successful you are at your job, or how well your children behave. Being comes from the internal realm. It has to do with how you view yourself and the world. It comes from the energy field of love and truth and has nothing to do with finite, material things. The being aspect of yourself doesn't care how much money is in your bank account, but instead cares about what type of character you have. Being encompasses intangibles such as spiritual growth, peace, bravery, and insight. When you are being, your actions align with your higher self.

Living a life of right action isn't just about *doing* right actions; it is also about right *being*. The Law of Sobriety says you must do estimable acts, such as creating a lifestyle that puts recovery first and foremost. But as you gain ground in your recovery, your sense of being will begin to know what right action looks like. Right action will come easily and naturally to you. You will know what actions support your recovery and what actions will destroy it. Remember, what you focus your attention on determines what you create or manifest in your life. How you invest the energy of your life force shapes your quality of life. If you make choices that conflict with your true being, there will be a disconnect. Suddenly, the actions you are taking don't match your deepest desires.

The process of "flow" occurs when your consciousness matches your goals, allowing psychic energy to flow smoothly, according to Mihaly Csikszentmihalyi, a professor and former chairman of the Department of Psychology at the University of Chicago. You are not in the flow when you are behaving in a way that makes you feel guilt, shame, anxiety, or fearfulness. However, when you are in the flow, your actions are natural, fluid, and graceful. Everything just feels "right." Csikszentmihalyi writes in *Flow: The Psychology of Optimal Experience,* "It is when we act freely, for the sake of the action itself rather than for ulterior motives, that we learn to become more than what we were."

Unclutter

Clutter is one of the things than can block us from achieving our goals. Clutter can take many forms—physical, mental, or emotional. Letting things accumulate without sorting through them (and without either getting rid of them or putting them in their place) is a perfect example of mindless action. Clearing out the clutter in our lives helps us live a life of right action.

Clearing out the physical clutter is every bit as important as sorting through the mental and emotional clutter. Objects can have powerful associations for us, and holding on to an object can be a symbol of holding on to a behavior or an idea. An obvious example might be holding on to cocktail glasses or drug paraphernalia. A less obvious example might be things given to us by a person who hurt us deeply. These things remind us of unhappiness, and when we hold on to them, we also hold on to the behaviors and memories associated with them.

I had one client who could not get rid of old photos of herself that were taken when she was in relationships that had ended poorly. Every time she looked at them, the photos would rekindle a sense of failure and loss. It was as if she

Unclutter *(cont'd from page 149)*

was addicted to those feelings. Although they were painful, these were the feelings she was used to and comfortable with. As crazy as that sounds, addicts and alcoholics get used to feelings of discomfort, and when things start to feel good, that's when they feel uncomfortable. They resort to old behaviors, feelings, and, of course, old habits. Be aware of that pity party you are used to throwing for yourself. Notice it and move on. It will only cause you misery—which is what you are learning to move away from when you embrace the Law of Sobriety.

Clearing out the clutter includes simply getting your home organized and in order. It's far easier to live a well-planned life of right action when you live in a well-ordered environment. Clutter of all types is negative energy, and when it fills our lives, it crowds out the positive energy. Get rid of the clutter to make room for positive energy to flow.

Another client I worked with could not get rid of old magazines, mail, or newspapers. She believed if she got rid of them, she would miss reading something important. By clinging to these old objects, her house was a mess—but they also kept her clinging to old thoughts and behaviors. Her worrying caused negative energy to circulate and recirculate, keeping her stuck and unwilling to move forward in her recovery. We formulated a plan to get rid of these things over weeks, months, and, eventually, years. When the clutter was gone, her worrying vanished, freeing her to breathe once again. She could now fully take in all the gifts her sobriety had to offer. She was able to create an art studio in the space she had cleared out and began to paint again, which was something she had stopped doing years ago when her disease took over.

Start by looking around your home and making a plan about where you'd like everything to go. This might be the time to rearrange the furniture or change what goes into which closet. Think about what you'll need to get the job done—maybe file folders or storage boxes—and go get them. Have a bin for things to throw away and another one for things to give away. As soon as each bin gets full, empty it: the throwaways into the trash and the giveaways to whatever charity you want to support. You can always find a sober living facility or a Salvation Army branch that can use items you no longer need or want.

If tackling the clutter in your home seems overwhelming, break it down into smaller tasks and set some interim goals. Can you organize one room in your home on a Saturday? If that's too much, can you organize one desk or chest of drawers? If even that seems too daunting, then organize just one drawer at a time. Put it on a schedule, so you organize one drawer a day until all the drawers are cleaned out and clutter free. When you finish that piece of furniture, move on to the next one. It doesn't matter how long it takes you to unclutter, as long as you keep moving forward.

Remember to give yourself credit every step of the way. Enjoy the space you've just uncluttered, no matter how small, and promise yourself to keep it that way.

TAPPING IN TO MOTIVATION

One of the most common reasons people don't achieve their goals is because they procrastinate. Procrastinating is not doing—it's putting off the doing until some later time. People procrastinate for a multitude of reasons. Some don't follow through on their actions because they can't tolerate being uncomfortable; others resent tasks that don't make them feel good immediately. And some people are easily distracted. They fool themselves into thinking some other activity is more important than the task they are working on. They may rationalize, "If I can't do this thing perfectly, then why do it at all?" This kind of all-or-nothing thinking is only an excuse to justify giving in to the temptation to do nothing.

Here's an example of all-or-nothing thinking: Perhaps your goal is to exercise five times a week but you can't get to the gym on Tuesday. You tell yourself, "I can't reach my goal this week, so why bother?" and you don't exercise at all. In fact, you could have taken a walk or done some simple stretching at home on Tuesday and still met your goal. But when you rationalize, it's all or nothing—usually nothing.

In his book *Emotional Intelligence*, psychologist Daniel Goleman says that research shows adults who were able to resist temptation by the age of four tend to be more "socially competent, personally effective, self-assertive, and better able to cope with the frustrations of life." Reading that the other way, people who were unable to resist temptation as children tend to be less socially competent, less effective, less assertive, and less able to cope with frustration. Sound familiar? Addicts and alcoholics usually have no patience and must learn to be comfortable in their own discomfort and understand that not every activity needs to feel good. In fact, there might even be pain involved. Pain, however, can be positive, giving you the energy you need to move forward. It is imperative not to get stuck in the pain, though, or use drugs and alcohol to avoid the pain. It is the moving through the pain that helps you grow and gain the self-esteem you need to both complete the smallest tasks and reach your fullest potential.

Why We Put Things Off

There have been many studies done on why we procrastinate and what the consequences are. Since psychological studies are mainly conducted at universities, most of the studies involve procrastinating about coursework. But the findings of these studies have broader implications.

A study published in *Psychological Science* in 1997 compared students who procrastinated with those who didn't. It found that early in the semester, procrastinators reported experiencing less stress and less illness. But later in the semester, they reported more stress and more illness, and overall, they were sicker. They also received lower grades. The researchers concluded that procrastinating is a self-defeating behavior that is marked by short-term benefits and long-term costs.

People who procrastinated also tended to attribute any success they had to luck or circumstances, rather than their own hard work, according to a 2000 study in the *Journal of Social Behavior & Personality*. The study also found that fear of failure and being a perfectionist were frequent causes of procrastination, especially in women.

A 2002 study published in the *European Journal of Personality* found that procrastinators were students who were highly motivated but were unable to resist temptations or ward off distractions while they studied. They intended to study more, but simply could not resist the lure of doing something fun. Several other studies also found that impulsiveness and being easily distracted are characteristics of procrastinators.

Tools for Change
Stop Procrastinating

One way to stop procrastinating and move forward with your goals or tasks is to imagine how your life would look in the future if you had never procrastinated about your responsibilities or aspirations.

Close your eyes, take a full breath in and a full breath out. Notice yourself at an earlier time in your life. What was it that you were passionate about but never risked trying? Was it writing, painting, skiing? What career path did you avoid because others persuaded you not to do it? Did you want to be an actor or a musician? What about when you decided it was too difficult to take that college entrance exam? Where would you be today if you had showed up that day to take that test?

These scenarios are not meant to shame you or cause you remorse. They are a reminder that you need not avoid anything anymore because you are afraid or it seems too difficult. Go ahead and imagine what you can do right now that you have been putting off. Visualize it, perhaps journal about it, and tomorrow take one step toward achieving it.

Another way to push yourself from procrastinating to doing is to take a look at those things you were willing to do in your active addiction and examine how you were able to accomplish them. You were able to panhandle for change and score your drugs for your next fix or concoct elaborate lies, weren't you? Take that same energy and put it toward something meaningful, positive, and purposeful. Remember how much you wanted to use drugs or alcohol? Now think about what you want to accomplish in your sobriety, and use the memory of that energy to drive you to get it done.

Another approach is to examine what your mental state and mood were when you did complete a task. What were you feeling as you got yourself going? How did you feel as you were doing the task? How did you feel about yourself afterward? How can you tap into those feelings to motivate yourself to do more? You can complete any task as long as you persevere and are single-minded about what needs to be done.

Resilient people are able to move forward with their goals without letting misfortune or difficulties affect them. They are able to see that any forces in their way are only temporary. Resilient people are positive and do not view any task as too difficult to work through. The exercise on the previous page will help you stop procrastinating. Another way to reach your goals is to look at the consequences of your behavior. If you act out impulsively and just react to what you are feeling without thinking, you can be sure you will suffer the consequences. But you need not be a victim of your impulses. If feelings are what motivate you, it is important to look at each one of them. Are you feeling fearful? Angry? Sad? What behaviors do you act out when you have each of these feelings?

Discovering how you can best cope with these feelings is the secret to right action. How can you take care of yourself when you are angry? What is your game plan? Maybe you need to do something physical, such as work out or go for a run, to decrease some of your rage. Maybe you need to practice loving-kindness when you are resentful. Maybe you need to call a friend or sponsor when you are feeling depressed. Maybe you need to examine and work through your fears so you can handle scary situations effectively. Maybe there is a spiritual solution to dealing with your fears.

This brings us back to planning. You need the time and the space to make the best decisions. Without them, you are once again acting on impulse, just as you did when you were using or drinking. Take the time to think about and plan how you will cope when you feel the things that used to defeat you. You must take your ego out of the equation when you are challenged by life. Let go of that obstinate nature and realize that there may be many solutions to keep you on the path toward fulfilling your goals.

Maybe you are being too judgmental of yourself or others, and this is what's keeping you from doing what you need to do. In Chapter 5 we learned how powerful it can be to imagine things from another person's point of view. This is true when you are trying to forgive others, but it's also true when you're trying to find the path of right action. Narcotics Anonymous, another twelve-step program, advises, "To gain a better understanding of how we may have harmed people, we may want to put ourselves in their shoes." Try to intentionally shift your awareness to how another person might be looking at the same situation. By looking at something from a different point of view, you open yourself up to an array of possibilities for accomplishing the same goals. Be open and willing to let the Law of Sobriety work so you can hear what the universe is trying to tell you. Your inner wisdom knows the way when you are stuck, are in fear, or just can't get out of your own way.

There is a vitality, a life force, a quickening that is translated through you into action, and because there is only one you in all time, this expression is unique. And if you block it, it will never exist through any other medium and will be lost. The world will not have it. It is not your business to determine how good it is or how valuable it is or how it compares with other expressions. It is your business to keep it yours, clearly and directly, to keep the channel open.

—Martha Graham

Achieving your goals can simply mean starting with the basics: learning to eat right, get enough rest, and exercise. (In addition to being good for you, these are great stress-busters.) Take a look at your relationships. Are they supporting your recovery or enabling your disease? Do you have any legal issues that need to be resolved? Are your finances in order? Is your spiritual program up to par? Learning to master the smallest of actions is right action. Sometimes we can only muster enough energy to do one small task. But you will be surprised at how much of your life is built on accomplishing just one thing at a time. Those pint-size successes can grow to be huge accomplishments. The point is to begin where you are with that first step—right now. When you believe it, your thoughts will mobilize you into action, and the Law of Sobriety says your belief will attract the energy you need to see that action through.

Living a life of right action does not mean you have to struggle or become obsessed with outcomes. Once you know what your goals are and have a plan for achieving them, your creative energy will take over and help you tackle things all the way. Remember, nothing is permanent, and change is always possible. Be compassionate with yourself as you go through this journey, and keep in mind that even the most inconsequential steps you take may be your greatest lessons.

Life is difficult. This is a great truth, one of the greatest truths. It is a great truth because once we truly see this truth, we transcend it. Once we truly know that life is difficult—once we truly understand and accept it—then life is no longer difficult. Because once it is accepted, the fact that life is difficult no longer matters.

—From *The Road Less Traveled* by M. Scott Peck

Tools for Change
Finding Your Path to Right Action

This is a meditation for living a life of right action. The purpose of this meditation is to gain insight into what will lead you to the right action.

- Sit in a comfortable position. Take several deep breaths.

- Allow yourself to receive whatever images, feelings, or thoughts arise from this meditation. Imagine there's a door in front of you and on the other side of the door the answers will be revealed to you—but first you must pose the questions.

- Decide exactly what you want to learn from this meditation. Here are some questions you might ask yourself to determine whether your decisions are in line with a life of right action.

✓ Are the decisions I am making matching my deepest desires?

✓ Are the decisions I am making fulfilling me?

✓ Are my actions creating joy from within myself or am I doing things to please others?

✓ Do the decisions I am making support my recovery?

✓ What is one small step I can take toward achieving my greatest desire?

✓ If I could make three changes that would significantly improve my recovery plan, what would they be?

✓ What is it that allows me to act out impulsively without thought to my actions?

✓ How am I rationalizing and justifying my actions in ways that are leading me further away from my sobriety?

✓ What are my greatest fears that are keeping me immobilized, stuck, and resistant to living a life of right action?

When you are clear about the answers you have received, create affirmations that align with your goals and desires. It may be easier for you to take the necessary steps if you break up your affirmations into smaller statements of purpose.

✓ I am making decisions in my life that align with my deepest desires.

✓ The decisions I am making are fulfilling and purposeful.

✓ The action steps I am taking bring me joy from within.

✓ I am learning to make decisions that are life-enhancing and support my recovery.

✓ One small step I can take toward achieving my greatest desires is to not procrastinate.

✓ Three changes that will significantly improve my recovery plan are to keep my promises, commit to an action plan, and be aware of the consequences of my behavior.

✓ I will no longer rationalize and justify my inability to commit so that I don't stray from my sobriety.

✓ My actions will be thought out with patience and integrity so that I do not act on my impulses.

✓ I will move forward no matter what and realize my fear of failing is just a thought and is not based on any reality.

SEVEN

Living with Awareness and Mindfulness

---

*Mindfulness is the miracle by which
we can call back our dispersed mind and restore it to
wholeness so that we can live each minute of life.*
—From *The Miracle of Mindfulness*
by Thich Nhat Hanh

Mindfulness means being aware only of the moment you are in, without thinking about the past or the future or getting caught up in opinions or judgments about what's going on. In other words, if you're eating an orange, all you notice is how the orange feels, smells, and tastes. If you're walking down the street, you pay attention to what it feels like to walk and what you notice along the way, but you don't think about anything else and don't judge anything you see.

Addicts and alcoholics tend to find it quite difficult to stay in the present moment. Often, they've had a history of trauma and they disassociate from the present or numb their pain with their addictions—if not drugs and alcohol, then other addictive behaviors. They fill their lives with things to keep themselves "busy"; if they're not busy, they are most likely worrying about the future or the past and waiting for some momentary, fleeting event that will take them out of their despair. That moment goes by like a flash, and the sadness that brought them to their addiction returns. When this happens, they become irritable, disappointed, frustrated, and sometimes think of themselves as victims—of just about everything.

Sometimes clients will ask me, "I'm sober now, so why am I still so miserable?" They're miserable because they are not living in the present moment; rather, they are living in a sense of not having something—and they don't even know what that something is! They have a chronic emptiness that can only be filled by living in the present moment. There is nothing to worry about in a single moment of time because in that moment there is no past and no future. The Law of Sobriety says you should direct your energy into simply being in the present; when you do, you realize that each moment you are doing exactly what you are meant to be doing. If you want to know how your recovery is going, look at how you are living the principles of the Law of Sobriety at this moment, right now.

When addicts or alcoholics are using, they build up a tolerance to the substance they are abusing and need more and more to achieve the feeling they seek. Unfortunately, the newly sober are often unable at first to feel pleasure in their sobriety, and they seek more stimulation the same way they sought more drugs or alcohol. But according to the Law of Sobriety, when you feel you are missing something, you are. When you radiate the energy of abundance, you receive everything sobriety has to offer. When you achieve your sobriety, joy and happiness are no longer blocked, and that empty longing for external gratification will fade away.

When my clients live in the present, they make decisions with clarity and are less impulsive. One client told me how he used to experience road rage. He would be so frustrated by other drivers cutting in front of him or not allowing him to pass that he'd start hunting for the nearest liquor store. He felt he couldn't continue without a drink to quell his terrible rage. Once he became sober, he realized he could live in the moment exactly the way it presented itself—whether it was a good moment or a bad one—without responding in extremes or having to numb himself. He realized that driving didn't need to be a roller coaster ride full of danger, but rather could be an experience that would unfold as it was supposed to. He no longer needed to fight what he was experiencing, because the fight only triggered his desire to drink.

When you loosen up your need to control every moment and just live in each moment instead, the Law of Sobriety takes over, giving you more energy to be at peace with each moment as it unfolds—even when that moment is uncomfortable. The Law of Sobriety enables you to lean into discomfort rather than push it away.

ATTENTION AND PURPOSE

My favorite definition of mindfulness is from the book *Wherever You Go, There You Are* by Jon Kabat-Zinn, founding director of the Stress Reduction Clinic and the Center for Mindfulness in Medicine, Health Care, and Society at the University of Massachusetts Medical School. Kabat-Zinn says, "Mindfulness means paying attention in a particular way: on purpose, in the present moment, and nonjudgmentally . . . Mindfulness provides a simple but powerful route for getting ourselves unstuck, back in touch with our own wisdom and vitality."

This definition strikes a chord on so many levels of recovery. To gain a better understanding of how and why, let's look deeper into the parts of this definition. What does it mean to pay attention in a particular way on purpose? It means consciously paying attention to each moment, from the smallest details of life, such as walking and eating, to the larger goals, such as your career, your personal relationships, and your recovery program. Living mindfully is living your life fully in each moment, with intention, meaning, value, authenticity, gratitude, and right action.

Living mindfully on purpose is all about a life fully lived with each breath you take. Each moment is meaningful and joyful because you are being the authentic person you are meant to be. All the choices and actions you take are done thoughtfully, with your values and goals at the forefront of your mind. Living mindfully on purpose enables you to live in gratitude each and every moment in whatever way the moment unfolds. The energy of mindfulness emerges when you stop grasping for whatever you think you don't have and accept what you do have right now, in this very moment.

We can seek choices thoughtfully, in ways that are consistent with what we want in life. The way we choose to live the next moment is the way we live the rest of our lives.

—From *Falling Awake*
by Dave Ellis

LIVING IN THE PRESENT MOMENT

Getting back to Kabat-Zinn's definition of mindfulness, what does it mean to live your life in the present moment? When you are an addict, you escape living in the moment with a temporary high, which, in essence, deadens your being. In that altered state, you have missed the moment. You have missed your child's smile, a dog wagging his tail, a sweet scent, the song of a bird. You can never recapture any of those moments; each one is forever in the past. And so are you—your inability to live in the moment comes from your obsession with living in the past. You numb yourself to push away past hurts and fears, and so you are never able to see what the present has to offer.

If you are immobilized by fear, anger, sadness, or impending doom, you have lost the moment to an array of emotions that will only reinforce your addictions and your self-destructive behaviors. Yes, there have been times in your life when you needed to escape from the moment—maybe a childhood trauma or an abusive relationship. But now is the time to live mindfully and in the present, experiencing the joys of life—and yes, even the lows of life—in a way that is palatable. Palatable does not mean easy, but it does mean simple.

Buddhists believe the only thing that keeps us from joy is the way we think. If we constantly evaluate everything around us, judging how much pleasure or pain those things bring us, we will never be satisfied. It is this distorted thinking that keeps addicts from being comfortable in their own skins. When we give up our attachments to endless pleasures, we are able to live comfortably, moment to moment, simply experiencing our lives as they unfold.

Mindful acceptance is a stance toward life. Watching the struggle without judging it, feeling the pain without drowning in it, and honoring the hurt without becoming it.

—From *The Mindfulness and Acceptance Workbook for Anxiety*
by John P. Forsyth and Georg H. Eifert

OBSERVING WITHOUT JUDGING

Being mindful means observing your thoughts without getting stuck in them. Our minds often dwell on the past or obsess about the future instead of focusing on the present. They create false stories that bear no truth to what is really going on. It is your mind that tells you you're bad, you're not good enough, you will never succeed, you won't find a job, a career, love, and that you can't get or stay sober. These false stories are not based in anything happening at the present moment. They come from a mind that is wandering around wildly in the past and future and judging everything it sees.

I vividly recall writing the proposal for this book to present to my publisher. My wild, wandering mind kept telling me, "The publisher will never go for this book idea" and "My ideas have been turned down in the past, so why should this proposal be any different?" I struggled with these thoughts, but instead of ignoring them, pushing them down, or burying them, I noticed them mindfully—with curiosity and profound compassion for myself. I knew that past disappointments were keeping me from staying in the present moment. I reminded myself that the publisher had not yet seen my proposal and there was no reason to assume it would be rejected. My mind was making up stories that assumed a negative outcome. When I examined these thoughts mindfully, I could see they were not based on anything that was actually happening in the present. I observed the thoughts and then moved on without judging myself. (And since you are reading this book right now, it is quite apparent that my mind *was* making up a false story. I'm certainly glad I chose to ignore those negative thoughts!)

The world we have created is a product of our thinking. It cannot be changed without changing our thinking.

—Albert Einstein

Peter's Story

Peter wanted to apply to several graduate schools, but he never actually did so because he was convinced he could not pass the entrance exams he needed to take. Worse, he was continuing to use drugs to drown out the fears that were crippling him. He had promoted his fears to the status of reality. I suggested he look at the fears straight on, acknowledge them, label them "fears," and let them go.

In his moments of mindful awareness, Peter realized that his thoughts were just temporary intrusions that were keeping him stuck in his disease. He could even see that the thoughts allowed him to make excuses to use drugs and not study for the exams. The stories his mind had made up were controlling his life. Peter was acting on his fear rather than on his reality, because he was living in his head rather than in the moment.

Obviously, Peter needed to learn how to stop giving his negative thoughts so much power. As he started to mindfully observe his mind and body when he had those thoughts, and was able to do so without making judgments, he noticed something: when he was anxious, he could feel a lump in his throat and tightness in his chest, and when he was optimistic he could feel his chest and throat opening. He noticed that his physical sensations and his thoughts were constantly changing. He realized that his mind was always racing ahead of his reality.

Once Peter was aware of the physical sensations, he could use them as reminders to also be mindful of his thoughts. For him, it meant noticing that his fears were just fears—nothing more, nothing less. This realization enabled him to tap into the Law of Sobriety by living in the moment, without falling prey to his self-defeating thoughts. As soon as he let go of all that negative energy, he became filled with positive energy, and he could start working toward his goals with a sense of purpose and determination.

The Danger of Positive Judgments

We have seen how negative judgments can paralyze us. But we also need to be mindful of positive judgments, which can be just as dangerous as negative ones. Depression and anxiety can appear when we make certain kinds of assumptions about ourselves, people, places, and things. Some examples are, "When I get sober, my life is going to be perfect," or "If I go to rehab, my parents will pay for my car," or "I don't understand why my spouse is still upset about my past behavior; I'm sober now." These positive judgments take you away from where you are right now, and if you live in them, you will only be disappointed.

These judgments can be dangerous because they are caused by impulsiveness, viewing yourself as a victim, or blaming others. When you struggle with thoughts of what you don't have, you move yourself closer and closer to your addictions. Serenity eludes you in these moments of desperation.

An important part of being nonjudgmental is considering whether you are setting impossible expectations for yourself. Maybe you are becoming impatient and feel things are just not moving along fast enough. Or possibly you are feeling sorry for yourself. When you are frozen with anxiety or are feeling stuck, ask yourself, "What am I feeling right now?" Mindfully scan your body and ask yourself, "What is my body trying to tell me? What or who am I avoiding? What or who am I not accepting?" When you learn to acknowledge your fears, you are accepting *you*. You are opening yourself up to the vulnerabilities that have kept you in the darkness.

Being nonjudgmental is about being profoundly accepting of yourself and others. When you accept yourself, others, and situations you are powerless to change, freedom begins. Acceptance enables you to let unforgiving thoughts pass through you rather than define you. Buddhists believe that insight comes when you are open to your thoughts without judgment. You don't dwell on the judgments your mind makes or allow them to close the door on your life. You view them instead with curiosity and know those thoughts are just thoughts—nothing more.

MINDFULNESS AND BREATHWORK

When you are not in a mindful place, your body and thoughts are disconnected. They are detached from one another, rather than being part of a whole, integrated system. When you practice mindfulness, you can learn to reconnect the body and the mind. The medium for this is your breathing. When you focus on your breath rather than the anxieties of your thoughts, you silence the stories in your head and live totally in the now.

There are many types of breathwork that will help you unite mind and body and cultivate mindfulness. One of the oldest is pranayama, the breathwork exercises of yoga. *Prana* means "life force" or "life energy" and *yama* means "discipline" or "control." So pranayama is really a technique for controlling your life energy. The *Hatha Yoga Pradipika,* a fifteenth-century yoga manual, says, "When the Breath wanders, the mind is unsteady, but when the Breath is still, so is the mind still."

The use of yoga breathing to effectively treat stress, anxiety, and depression was reported on in a 2005 study done at the Columbia College of Physicians and Surgeons in New York. The researchers, Richard Brown, M.D., and Patricia Gerbarg, M.D., documented the effects yoga breathing has on the body, including changes in the brain and the endocrine system. They also found that yoga breathing techniques "can alleviate anxiety, depression, everyday stress, post-traumatic stress, and stress-related medical illnesses." They found that regular practice offered the best results to "enhance well-being, mood, attention, mental focus, and stress tolerance."

Pranayama

There are many traditional yoga breathing techniques, and they're all based on understanding what it means to take a complete breath. A complete breath involves the entire respiratory system and expands the lungs to their fullest capacity. When you inhale a complete breath, the breath fills your collarbone, then the upper part of the lungs, then the rib cage, then the lower part of the lungs, then the abdomen. When you exhale, the breath empties from you in the reverse order.

Pranayama is done through the nose, with the mouth and eyes gently closed. When you are first learning the complete breath, it can be helpful to practice while lying down. Rest one hand gently on the chest and one on the abdomen, so you can feel the rise and fall of each part as you inhale and exhale fully.

At its simplest, pranayama can just be a series of complete breaths. You inhale slowly and completely, hold the inhalation for a moment, exhale slowly and completely, hold the empty lungs for a moment, and repeat. Lengthening and then holding the exhalation is relaxing, while lengthening and holding the inhalation is energizing. A balanced breathing pattern helps you feel more balanced and less stressed.

For example, to increase energy you might inhale while

counting slowly to six, hold the inhalation for four counts, exhale while counting slowly to four, and hold the exhalation for one count. To relax, you might inhale while counting slowly to six, hold the inhalation for one count, exhale while slowly counting to eight, and hold the exhalation for four counts. To balance yourself, you might inhale for six, hold for two, exhale for six, and hold for two again. (You should think of these numbers as relative ratios. Don't force your breath or struggle to keep to the counts. As you practice, it will be easier to extend each breath for a longer period of time.)

Pick the breathing pattern that suits the state your body and mind are in at the moment, and repeat it over and over. Start with just five minutes. You will be amazed at the change that comes over you. These complete breaths cleanse and reconnect the body and mind. They bring you into mindfulness because you are focusing solely on your breathing in the present moment.

In times of extreme stress, alternate nostril breathing can restore your emotional balance. Place your right thumb on your right nostril and your right middle finger on your left nostril. Use your thumb to gently press your right nostril until it is closed. Inhale for six through your left nostril only. Hold for two while you release your thumb and use your middle finger to gently close your left nostril. Exhale for six through your right nostril, hold for two, then inhale for six through your right nostril. Hold for two while you release your middle finger and use your thumb to gently close your right nostril. So the pattern is: inhale through the left, hold, exhale

Pranayama *(cont'd from page 171)*

through the right, hold, inhale through the right, hold, exhale through the left, hold.

If you're in a public place where you really can't sit with your hand on your nose, you can imagine you are practicing alternate nostril breathing. Simply sit quietly and imagine the alternate nostril pattern while you take controlled, complete breaths.

A good place to learn more about yoga breathing techniques is http://www.abc-of-yoga.com/pranayama.

MINDFULNESS AND RELAPSE

Just as we observe our thoughts without judgment, we must do the same with our actions. So often in sobriety, one slip can mean being addicted again for years and years. By seeing the relapse for what it is—just a relapse—it becomes much easier to begin sobriety anew. Many clients of mine see a slip as a complete failure and an excuse to keep on using. A relapse is simply a mistake. When you call yourself a "loser" or a "failure" for using again, there can't be any learning or growth.

For example, I have a client who is learning to set boundaries in her relationship as part of her therapy. She is learning to communicate with her husband in a new way, but sometimes this causes her discomfort and anxiety. She has noticed that when her husband is verbally abusive, she heads for the pantry. She swallows her feelings along with bars and bars of chocolate. Dealing with her uncomfortable feelings has caused her to overindulge. Sometimes she can sit with the physical and emotional sensations of anxiety, but other times she numbs them with chocolate. Does this mean she is a complete failure? Absolutely not. She is learning new ways to cope. There may be setbacks, but mindfulness enables us to notice these setbacks with curiosity rather than judgment. If you relapse, you can use the same mindful approach to view yourself and what has happened.

One way to view a relapse is to detach yourself from the emotional content and just be curious about it. As a neutral observer, what do you see? What was it that brought you back to using? Instead of judging yourself harshly, observe what your triggers were when you relapsed and set an intention to avoid those triggers in the future, rather than letting yourself be swallowed up by them.

No matter what the reason was for your relapse, it's time to slow down and observe the relapse and its causes, rather than hiding from it or judging yourself harshly. When you hide from something you are afraid of, you are abandoning yourself, according to the Law of Sobriety. When you wake up to what you fear, transformation is possible. You can learn new ways to deal with situations that have mystified you. When you face the fears that have imprisoned you, you can learn to respond in appropriate ways, rather than being reactive or impulsive.

I suspect that harsh self-judgment begins with our sense of competition and inferiority. Not only do we read about the ideal family life in the handbook, we delude ourselves into thinking that our neighbor actually leads that life.

—From *The Clenched Fist or Guiding Hand of Self Judgment*
by Rabbi Jill Madere

Coping with Cravings

People who are new to sobriety can experience terrible cravings. If you go to twelve-step meetings, it's something you'll almost always hear the newcomers talk about. They crave everything from the drugs and alcohol to the rituals that went along with their using and drinking. They miss the beautiful crystal wine glasses they used to drink from, or preparing the crack pipe for their next hit. The whole ritual is romanticized from start to finish. They crave the high drama and the excitement of getting away with their destructive behaviors.

The forceful energy of cravings can be enormous. One way to cope is by being mindful of the cravings, rather than resisting them. By allowing the cravings to just be, you remove the need to resist them. Watch them mindfully and without judgments. Just know them for what they are. You realize that cravings don't define you or whether you will stay sober. They are just there.

When you see cravings as just another aspect of your recovery, you can better understand the strength of your disease and develop a deep compassion for yourself. Noticing this aspect of yourself ultimately leads you to freedom. You no longer need immediate solutions to cope with your cravings—the way you needed an instant fix when you were using. Noticing your urges rather than acting on them gives you back your life.

Mindfulness is a very important part of avoiding relapse, because a relapse is about being less than fully aware at the time it happens. When you relapse, all the new behaviors you have learned in recovery disappear. You forget that negative feelings such as rage, shame, depression, and fear are triggers for your addiction. Instead of doing what you have learned to do, using the Law of Sobriety as your compass (such as calling someone when you have these despondent feelings or viewing these feelings dispassionately), you fall victim to your negative feelings.

This is when the precious pause of mindfulness is invaluable. By taking that pause, you have the opportunity to stop the habitual behaviors that led to your addiction. By being mindful, you don't deny your feelings, shut your feelings down, try to numb them, or hope they will go away. Instead, you acknowledge your uncomfortable feelings without judgment. Then you come up with solutions to deal with them.

THE NEGATIVITY ADDICTION

Bill's Story

Bill was going through a divorce from his manipulative and abusive wife. Even after they reached a settlement, she repeatedly threatened to take him back to court or take their children and leave the country. Abuse was nothing new to Bill; his father had beaten both him and his mother. Bill received very little nurturing from his mother because she herself was caught up in the domestic violence and was unable to be emotionally present for him. Intermittently, his paternal grandmother provided him with some emotional support, but it was rare.

Bill grew up devastated by the emotional and physical abuse he had suffered, and ultimately married a woman who continued to traumatize him in the same way his parents had. Eventually, his wife left him for another man. Bill feared he would never deserve happiness. He was frozen with anxiety that his ex-wife would take his children from him or convince them not to have anything to do with him. Under a shared custody agreement, Bill was able to be a good father to his children, and they loved being with him. But when they were not around, he would drink himself to sleep. He could not cope with the anxiety he felt about being abandoned.

Fortunately, Bill had a very good friend at work who supported him through this dark period in his life. His friend encouraged him to seek help, and Bill found himself in my office because he was suffering from depression, drinking, and suicidal thoughts.

In therapy, we talked about the fact that Bill was holding on to the anger he felt for his ex-wife, and that this anger was eating him up inside. As therapy progressed, he learned to accept the fact that his emotions were only temporary and that in time they would pass through him. When he felt anger toward his ex-wife, he learned how to forgive her in the moment, rather than lashing out at her, which would only have caused him more pain. He discovered that it was a lot easier to forgive one hurt in a single moment (something he could manage) than to forgive hundreds of hurts over years and years (something he was still struggling with). He worked on resisting the urge to respond to his ex-wife's abuse and threats.

When his anger resurfaced, Bill listened to the signals his body was sending. He noticed that his hands and jaw would clench and his stomach would tighten. These became his cues to pause and become aware of his physical sensations and notice his rage in a mindful way. Eventually, he learned to let the anger go. Bill came to realize his ex-wife was never going to change; instead, he needed to change his reactions to her. He let go of his thoughts that she should act in a certain way or be different—thoughts that just made him angrier and more hurt.

Bill realized that, in a way, he was addicted to his rage and pain. He thought about them all the time and his mind created scenarios where they would resurface, even when his ex-wife was not around. His path to sobriety included giving up those terrible mental addictions. He accepted the wisdom of his body, knowing true emotional pain comes and goes. In Alcoholics Anonymous it is said, "Pain is inevitable, but suffering is optional." By being mindful of his pain, Bill no longer suffered. He stopped clinging to beliefs that no longer served him. In time, his depression lifted, his drinking subsided, and he no longer thought about harming himself.

Do you have the patience to wait till the mud settles and the water is clear? Can you remain unmoving till the right action arises by itself?

—From *Tao Te Ching*
by Lao-tzu

The whispers of the universe can always be heard when you are not swallowed up by negative thoughts. When you are critical of yourself, don't buy into it—just notice it. The truth will reveal itself in these moments of contemplation. When anger arises, notice that, too. Insight is just around the corner when you cultivate the practice of mindfulness.

RETRAINING YOUR MIND

Emotional thoughts are a product of the amygdala, the region of the brain where emotional memory is stored and processed. When an emotional memory is triggered, your thoughts in the present moment are hijacked by a powerful memory from the past. Your reactions become a byproduct of these earlier memories. You don't even recognize that these emotions are in the past, not the present. So, for example, if your boss says, "Your sales could have been a little better this month. Let's work on ways to get those numbers up," it might trigger an extremely painful memory of your father telling you, "You never do anything right. I'm surprised you ever get anything done." You then react to your boss's mild critique and offer of help with the pain and rage you felt when your father criticized you so harshly.

Mindfulness is a way to rewire this old brain circuitry and replace it with reactions that are firmly rooted in your present reality. This is done by developing the ability to be consciously aware of your emotions and automatic thoughts. When you notice them without letting them take over, you make room for inner peace. Your emotions, negative feelings, and addictions lose their grip.

The Case for Mindfulness

There is a growing body of scientific evidence that practicing mindfulness can increase our enjoyment of life, improve our ability to cope with illness, and improve our physical and emotional health. In studies reported by the University of Massachusetts Medical School's Center for Mindfulness in Medicine, Health Care, and Society, mindfulness has been found to help reduce chronic pain and stress, and to speed healing.

The February 2004 issue of *Harvard Women's Health Watch* reported that learning to focus the mind can help you manage the stress of everyday living. And that makes a lot of sense because, at its core, mindfulness simply means doing only one thing at a time. Most of our time is spent doing dozens of things at the same time. For example, when we're washing the dishes, perhaps we're thinking about being resentful at having to do the dishes, what happened that day at work, the argument we had with someone the day before yesterday and what we should have said to them, whether there's anything in the house to eat for dessert, who chipped the new dishes, whether we actually like that dish pattern, how we are going to meet the next car payment, and so on. Imagine how much easier it would be to just notice the warm water and the scent of the dish soap and how the dishes feel in our hands. It would be a rest from all that mental noise and self-generated anxiety.

It's easy enough to direct your awareness anywhere you choose. But mindfulness takes practice. You need to remind yourself to stay in the moment you're in. The *Women's Health Watch* article offered some tips on how to achieve mindfulness in your everyday life. These include:

- When you're driving, pay attention to your breathing or your environment when you stop at red lights.
- Before you go to sleep and when you wake up, take some mindful breaths. Instead of allowing your mind to wander over the day's concerns, direct your attention to your breathing.
- Find a task that you do impatiently or unconsciously, such as standing in line or brushing your teeth, and concentrate on the experience.
- Make an everyday occurrence, such as answering the phone or buckling your seat belt, a reminder to return to the present. That is, think about what you're doing and observe yourself doing it.

Paula's Story

Paula felt tremendous rage toward her drug-addicted parents, especially her father. She told me that when social workers came to visit her home to check on the conditions, her father would force her to lie to them. He would threaten to beat her if she said anything that could get him into trouble. She knew her father was a drug dealer, and he was abusive both physically and verbally to her and her sisters, as well as extremely neglectful. But she could never reveal these things for fear of being severely punished. She described the situation as "crazy making."

I asked Paula what it might have felt like if there had been someone there to protect her from her father. She resisted the idea—resisted even imagining it. I pushed her again: "What if there had been someone in your life who could have made you feel safe and secure?" I asked her to be still with that thought, to observe the thought from a distance, rather than getting caught up in whether or not it was possible. Suddenly Paula's shoulders dropped and her eyes filled with tears. She let out a deep breath and told me how relieved she felt. "How wonderful it would have been if I could have just told the truth and someone really heard me and acknowledged my pain." She wiped away her tears of relief and realized that what she had been looking at all along were just thoughts. Her thoughts were under her control, and she could change them any time she wanted to.

She began to realize that her memories were just that—thoughts she could look at without reacting to them. They were recollections of past events, not reflections of her present reality. She could trust what she was feeling inside without having to get hooked by those negative emotions.

Paula had lived with some shame for lying to the social workers as a child. But when she looked at the situation in a mindful way, without the emotions she had always attached to it, she realized she hadn't done anything wrong. She was just a little girl frozen in fear. She was the victim, not the perpetrator, and could see things as they had actually happened. She didn't have to run from an unbearable present anymore; the present, although difficult, became easier as Paula became more mindful.

Cognitive Distortions

Cognitive distortions are distorted, negative ways of thinking. The first step in clearing out this kind of thinking is to recognize it. Psychologists recognize these ten as being the most common:

1. All-or-nothing thinking: You see things as black and white—total success or total failure.
2. Overgeneralization: You see a single event as an endless pattern.
3. Mental filter: You pick out a single negative detail and think only of that.
4. Disqualifying the positive: You reject positive experiences as irrelevant.
5. Jumping to conclusions: You interpret things negatively and assume everything will turn out badly.
6. Magnification or minimization: You exaggerate the importance of bad things and minimize the importance of good things.
7. Emotional reasoning: You assume your negative emotions reflect the way things really are.
8. "Should" statements: You try to motivate yourself and others using guilt.
9. Labeling and mislabeling: You negatively label yourself or others based on a single event.
10. Personalization: You see yourself as the cause of external events that you really had nothing to do with.

Tools for Change
Mindfulness and Your Addiction

One exercise for cultivating mindfulness is to list thoughts that come to your mind when you think of addiction. For example:

- When I think of my addiction, _____ comes to mind.
- When I think of my recovery, _____ comes to mind.
- The negative thoughts I have about my recovery include _____
  _____ .
- The positive thoughts I have about my recovery include _____
  _____ .
- A nonjudgmental thought about my addiction and recovery is ____
  _____ .
- I am willing to accept_____ about my addiction.
- Regarding my relapses, I get stuck in a story about _____
  But now I can allow those thoughts to move through me.
- I can replace my past way of thinking about _____
  with thinking in the present about _____ .

What makes mindfulness such an important tool for sobriety is that we have it with us always and can use it any time, anywhere. I often suggest to my clients that they pause frequently during the day to take mindful breaths or mindful walks. It is amazing how your "stories" of the day dissolve when you become attentive to them without getting pulled in by them. Bosses become more acceptable to you. Other people's moods become more tolerable. Annoying family members become more bearable. You realize that whatever is objectionable will pass. You don't take others on with defensive reactions anymore. Suddenly, these situations become learning opportunities.

You realize there are many perspectives on the same situation. You create distance from yourself while gaining a new point of view.

Ryan's Story

Ryan had several family members who were alcoholics. Ryan had been an alcoholic as well, but was now in recovery and living a sober life. Rather than enjoying his sobriety, though, he was completely absorbed in how the others in his family were living. He constantly judged them and lectured them on how they should be living their lives. Although he tried to be a model of a positive person in recovery, they just didn't get it. They were not ready.

Ryan was frustrated, angry, and annoyed, and could not let these feelings go. I asked him to take a few breaths and just notice what was happening in the moment at my office. What did it feel like as his feet touched the ground? When each vertebra in his spine lightly rested on the couch where he was sitting? What did he notice happening in his body as he felt the support of the cushion behind him? Ryan said he felt fairly calm and comfortable. I nudged him on, asking him to tell me what else he noticed. He used the words *expansive, empowered,* and *grounded.* Then I asked him to notice how he felt when he thought of his brother who could not get sober. He said he suddenly felt tightness in his gut. I asked him to name the feeling. He said he felt anxious. "And what does anxious feel like?" I asked. "It feels empty," Ryan replied. I asked him to stay present with that feeling and just let those sensations subside.

Stress is caused by being "here" but wanting to be "there," or being in the present but wanting to be in the future. It's a slit that tears you apart inside.

—From *The Power of Now* by Eckhart Tolle

After we finished, Ryan realized he no longer had to experience rage every time he thought about his brother. It was an automatic, mindless reaction. When he became mindful, he could stop having that reaction. He also realized that underneath the rage was fear that his brother would die—just as their father had died—from alcoholism. When Ryan became mindful of that fear, he no longer had to react to it. He developed more insight and saw other choices he could make in the way he dealt with his family. Ryan could shift from his automatic way of reacting toward his brother because he now understood that it was his own anxiety causing him to be angry. Being mindful gave him the freedom to "detach with love" (a concept encouraged by Al-Anon, a support program for friends and families of problem drinkers).

Detaching with Love

Sometimes you become so worried about another person's problems that you take those problems onto yourself. You become so involved in the other person's life that you lose a sense of yourself as a separate person. For example, if you know someone who is an addict or an alcoholic, you may decide not to go out at night so you can be available if that person needs a ride home or needs help in a dangerous situation. You stop living your own life because you are so worried about the addict or alcoholic.

But the reality is that you can't live someone else's life for him or her. You need to detach yourself—separate yourself, both emotionally and spiritually—from that person and recognize that sometimes nothing you say or do will make someone change.

> Detaching with love means recognizing that you still love the addict or alcoholic, but that you must remove yourself from the disease and its effects. You accept others exactly as they are, but refuse to get involved in their personal drama.

Mindfulness can be measured by how often you prevent negative emotions from dictating your reactions or crippling you. Buddhists regard getting stuck in harmful emotions as a major aspect of suffering, and what we know about the science of mindfulness bears this out. The Law of Sobriety says that the energy you put out into the universe, whether positive or negative, is exactly what you will receive. If your automatic emotional reactions are negative, negativity is what will come back to you. But if you gain awareness of your negative emotions in your mindfulness practice, they need not run the show. They are simply there and you observe them. Loosening your hold on negative thoughts and being fully present in each moment gets you back in touch with your "own wisdom and vitality," as Jon Kabat-Zinn wrote. Paying attention in the moment gets you back to who you are and what is truly happening in your life. Living on purpose then becomes the result of living mindfully and authentically.

If you practice mindfulness consistently, it becomes a habit. Your intention to practice daily will become a way of living. You can practice mindfulness informally (as described in the box on page 178) as simply a way to expand your awareness using everyday actions. Informal mindfulness means getting out of autopilot mode and getting into a mindful way of being, whether you are brushing your teeth, driving, getting out of bed, or waiting in line at the grocery store. Mindfulness is also part of formal meditation (as described in the exercise on page 187). Either way, as you become more mindful in your daily life, feelings of anger can soften into feelings of compassion. Depression can turn into determination. Fear can be replaced by forgiveness. Nothing needs to snag on the ocean floor when you allow your thoughts to drift naturally, effortlessly, and purposely. Mindfulness enables you to show up for life—the true life that you're living now. When you're mindful of your life, your actions become a choice rather than a mindless series of habitual behaviors. Only then can your energies be focused on a purposeful recovery.

Tools for Change
A Meditation to Cultivate Mindfulness

A formal mindfulness meditation begins by sitting or lying in a comfortable and supported position. Adjust yourself until you are completely comfortable in a position where you can remain completely still. Scan your body and notice whether you want to change or fix anything or are just embracing the experience as it is. Take several complete breaths. Use a breathing rhythm that is designed to relax or balance you.

As you breathe, notice any sensations that arise in your body. If you notice any areas of tightness, let the tension go. As thoughts come and go, observe them as if you were watching a movie. They are just thoughts. Watch them go by. They have no power and no emotional content.

To determine whether you are living with awareness and mindfulness, ask yourself the following questions:

- Am I paying attention to all of my senses?
- Am I looking at things from a new perspective?
- Am I practicing mindfulness skills by being aware of each experience moment by moment?
- Am I paying attention to my thoughts as they come and go without getting stuck in them?
- Am I learning to separate the areas of my life I can control and things I am powerless over?
- Am I able to observe inside of me that which is already whole and complete just as it is?
- Am I able in each moment to see rather than analyze what is going on within and around me with clarity and ease?

Once you have completed your formal or even informal mindfulness practice, create affirmations that support living your life with moment-to-moment awareness. These affirmations might include:

✓ Every moment in life is a gift and an opportunity to pay attention with awareness.

✓ I will listen to the still, silent voice of the universe as I make choices that support my recovery.

✓ I realize a relapse is just a relapse and is always an opportunity for me to learn and grow.

✓ I can slow down and take a pause rather than acting on my impulses and urges to use.

✓ I can notice my obsessions with kindness, compassion, and love and wait for them to pass through me.

✓ I will allow this moment to unfold as it is meant to be rather than try to fix, change, or control it.

✓ I observe my thoughts as just thoughts and no longer get stuck in them.

EIGHT

Learning to Let Go of
Resistance and Attachments

---

*At the precise moment you commit, the Divine
will touch you. Faith will activate your journey.
Patience will maintain it. Surrender will accomplish it.*

—From *Be Still and Know*
by Mara Marin

The final step of the Law of Sobriety is learning how to let go
of your attachment to the idea that your life ought to be a certain way,
and to let go of resistance to who you really are. When you live with
the Law of Sobriety as your guidepost, you are able to deal with whatever is in front of you because you are not attached to having things
turn out exactly as you imagined them. When you let go of the way
you believe things are supposed to be, you free yourself from negativity—the perpetual disappointment, doubt, and frustration that
come when things don't turn out as you thought they would. When
you let go of your attachment to a false sense of who you are and what
your life should be, you invite positive energy into your life.

What does it mean to resist the reality of who you are? If you continue believing that the next time you use drugs or drink the outcome will be different, you are refusing to accept the part of your true self that cannot control your alcohol or drug use. Instead, you are embracing a false self that does not embody your authentic nature. Acknowledging the reality of your disease is not a prison sentence, but rather a personal truth. The Law of Sobriety only works when you recognize your true self. Making the shift from wanting things to be different to being honest with yourself about how things truly are enables you to take actions that are constructive and energizing. Only when you make that shift can you attract all you desire in life.

Substance abusers have usually crossed the line into addiction when there are psychological, social, physiological, spiritual, and/or environmental consequences of their using. But even those consequences aren't enough to motivate most people to go to rehab or attend a twelve-step meeting. They wait until they have completely lost control or caused major havoc in their lives—until they have reached rock bottom. Most of the clients I've worked with in the Malibu rehab treatment centers and on *Celebrity Rehab* have reached what is the bottom for them. Typically, this means losing something of great value because of their addiction, such as a spouse, children, or a job. Sometimes it means experiencing financial devastation or serious legal issues.

The Celebrity's Story

I worked in private practice with a celebrity who was continually relapsing. He prioritized drug use over time spent with his family; his wife made family plans but he never participated, and he always missed his children's activities. He still had his singing career, his expensive car, and all the material success and possessions he could possibly want, but his wife was no longer willing to live with the situation.

He had lost his family's respect, but he refused to let go of his attachment to the idea that because he still had his money and possessions, he must not have a "real" problem. In the recovery community, we say he could not surrender to his disease. It means he could not stop fighting the reality that he had a problem.

This client had a huge case of denial. Alcoholism and drug addiction are the only diseases that convince people that they don't have a disease. This client truly believed he was not an addict because he was functional and had not lost anything he valued. This attitude made him resistant to help: who needs help when they think there isn't a problem? Yet he eventually learned that although he still had his money, every time he chose drugs over his children, he was losing his family's respect and hitting bottom all over again. When his family members began to set limits and boundaries and he came to realize he was losing his family, he was finally willing to surrender to his addiction—in other words, let go of his resistance to his reality. Once he did, the Law of Sobriety gave him the tools he needed to remain clean and sober.

Refusing to acknowledge who you truly are keeps you in a cycle of deceit and unhealthy behaviors, and according to the Law of Sobriety, this will only attract more deceit and unhealthy behaviors. The best way to break out of this cycle is to let go of your attachment to the stories you make up in your head and replace your unhealthy behaviors with healthy activities that nurture your soul. This will set you on the path to becoming who and what you desire to be. These healthy activities can include such things as journaling, mindfulness, exercise, meditation, prayer, attending twelve-step meetings, getting professional guidance, and replacing negative thoughts and emotions with positive ones. In the case of my celebrity client, it also included spending quality time with his family. This increased his sense of purpose and ultimately enabled him to place less importance on his material attachments. He finally realized that real joy came from his loving relationships rather than from material things, and that his material attachments were keeping him in his disease and apart from his family.

THE UNCOMFORTABLE EMBRACE

By admitting you have a problem with drugs or alcohol, you not only let go of your denial, but you make it possible to embrace what it means to be an alcoholic or addict. "Embrace" means to accept willingly and enthusiastically. Why would you want to embrace your disease? Because when you know your truth, then and only then can you take the actions necessary for your recovery.

It is important to realize that embracing your disease does not mean you are always going to feel comfortable. Simply saying out loud, "I am an alcoholic" or "I am a drug addict" can be extremely uncomfortable—especially if you have lived most of your life in denial. And recovery must include examining the events and misconceptions in your life that have gotten you to this point. Sitting down and examining all of your emotional pain, trauma, and baggage from the past can certainly be uncomfortable. After all, these are truths you have been numbing and suppressing for years.

Doreen's Story

You need to know that it is okay to feel uncomfortable with yourself in sobriety, and it is also okay to be uncomfortable in another person's discomfort. My client Doreen had a very low threshold for discomfort. Her young daughter would throw temper tantrums, and often Doreen would give in to her child's demands, no matter what they were, just to get her daughter to calm down. The child would get under Doreen's skin, and Doreen was not willing to experience any discomfort when her daughter was feeling frustrated and acting out. In an attempt to numb her own discomfort, Doreen would make the situation worse by turning to drugs, which were already a problem for her because of her poor coping skills.

In essence, Doreen was enabling her daughter's temper tantrums, and by doing so, her child did not learn how to regulate her own emotions. Later, the daughter developed her own drug problem. She had no coping skills when she became upset or frustrated. She believed she should have whatever she wanted, and Doreen's actions had taught her that if she acted out, she would get whatever she wanted. Her impulsiveness and her unwillingness to sit with uncomfortable feelings were two of the reasons she sought drugs to self-medicate. She had no ability to just tolerate discomfort for a bit and know that eventually it would pass. Of course, these were not the only reasons Doreen's daughter became an addict, but they were contributing factors. Obviously, throughout her life she faced many disappointments, as we all do. Her inability to cope with these disappointments was the beginning of her addiction. She used boys, shopping, food, and eventually drugs to soothe and escape her frustrations. She was living in a world of "it should be this way," making herself more unhappy by remaining attached to ideas and behaviors that didn't serve her.

My work with Doreen, and eventually with her daughter, was not only to teach them both healthy ways to self-soothe (such as relaxation skills, meditation, and journaling), but also to teach them how to accept discomfort without attaching a story to it. When you are uncomfortable about something that is not going right in your life, often the stories you create in your head are the cause of your emotional pain. These stories are just transient thoughts; they are not your reality. For example, you might really want the latest, greatest version of a multitasking cell phone but can't afford it. The story you create about it may say you can't get some vital task accomplished without it, or you can't be effective in your job or in your personal life. This story is not true, but you become attached to it and begin to believe you will never be happy without the device.

Once Doreen and her daughter learned to detach from the thoughts that frustrated them, rather than fighting them, shutting them down, or using drugs to numb them, they were able to surrender to their reality. They learned to notice their discomfort as simply thoughts and just let them go.

One of life's paradoxes is that in order to change an unwanted situation, we must first accept it the way it is. If you wish to move forward in your life, first make peace with what you are presently experiencing.

—From *Listening to Your Inner Voice*
by Douglas Bloch

THE ROLES WE PLAY

As I was writing this book, I found myself wondering just how successful it would be. Of course, no one can really answer that question. When I realized what I was doing, I fought those thoughts of needing to know, but at times I could not let them go. I used up a lot of mental energy creating elaborate scenarios and formulas in my head by which I thought I might predict my book's future. Other times, I got discouraged. I feared the book would not be well received, even when there was no way I could know this. All I did was cause myself endless frustration—which left me in no state to do any writing.

Eventually, I surrendered to the fact that what was going to unfold was out of my control. I realized I was letting old belief systems affect me in a negative way. Some of the belief systems that have haunted me throughout the years are, "I started too late in my career to ever really be successful" and "Everything always happens for others but not for me." Oh, do I despise that one! That is the victim mentality to the fullest. I have had to work very hard to let that one go, and to be perfectly honest, it still shows up occasionally to visit me like an uninvited guest.

While resonating so much negativity, how could I possibly receive anything positive from the universe? I recognized those unconstructive thoughts as saboteurs, so I tried instead to focus on what was before me, which was finishing this book. I realized my fears were taking up huge amounts of energy. Once I detached from the eventual outcome, I became more creative, resourceful, and enthusiastic about what I was doing in the here and now.

I realized that I had to stop defining my identity by my thoughts, feelings, and judgments about myself. There is nothing wrong with attributing purpose, values, and standards to oneself, but identifying with thoughts, feelings, and judgments that come and go is unrealistic and self-defeating. I am much more than the relative success of a published book, and you are so much more than the relative success of whatever you might attempt.

Many of my clients identify with their roles. Instead of identifying with their core self, they become their professions. This happens especially with people who have high-profile careers. They let their jobs as musicians, singers, athletes, actors, directors, or whatever their professions are, define them. If something is lost—for example, an important job or prestige in their industry—they begin to lose themselves.

My husband works as a television and film costume supervisor. When he had a serious accident and had to stay home to heal, he initially had trouble with letting go of "being" that profession. He's much more than that job; he is a loving husband, stepfather, son, grandson, uncle, brother, son-in-law, friend, and a beautiful soul. He is also a man in recovery. He is so much more to so many people in his life who love and need him. And all those things about him remained true, even when he wasn't working. "Television and film costume supervisor" is just a role he plays; it is not his authentic self.

We are what we think.
All that we are arises with our thoughts.
With our thoughts we make the world.
Speak or act with a pure mind
And happiness will follow you
As your shadow, unshakable.

—From *Dhammapada: The Sayings of the Buddha*

When you stop identifying yourself by the roles you play, you can be quite uncomfortable. While you are dismantling your false self, your true nature emerges, but that never happens without some pain. You have been hiding behind your actively addicted and alcoholic self; for a long time, that was your role. You need not attach to that identity anymore. You are now sober and in recovery, and that is who you are and who you are becoming. It's normal to grieve for your old identity and habits (no matter how destructive they may have been), but working through the Law of Sobriety, your new persona will emerge—the person you were always supposed to be. You were not created to just be a junkie or an alcoholic. Yes, you had to go through that process and learn important lessons, and yes, that is a part of you that cannot be erased, but you don't have to remain attached to it anymore.

When parts of your old persona reemerge, don't try to resist and don't be afraid. You are just shedding old destructive patterns, and they will soon be replaced with healthier ways of being. Just be mindful of these changes as they arise. There is no need to escape from yourself anymore. There is no need to be afraid. The universe and your higher power are watching your back. You are entering a new era of awakening. This new way of being allows you to respond in new and healthier ways while letting go of old habits of compulsiveness and obsession. The new you will unfold naturally as you embrace the Law of Sobriety.

CODEPENDENCY AND CONTROL

Another way we sometimes become the role we play is as a parent. How many parents have you met who view their children as an extension of themselves? What a responsibility it is to live up to your parents' expectations! What a burden to think that your parents' happiness depends on who you are or who you are becoming. That is a stepping-stone to codependent behavior.

Codependency is unhealthy emotional dependence. Children who feel they can never live up to their parents' expectations begin to think of themselves as perpetual victims. They learn not to trust other people, and they don't trust themselves. They try to constantly please others—no matter what it costs them—to avoid being emotionally abandoned. But that never really works because they don't feel they deserve the approval.

As an adult, a codependent person becomes caught up in how others view her and has no sense of self. If others express approval, she must be good. If others do anything that implies less than total approval, she must be bad. She depends on others to tell her what kind of person she is. This leaves little room for becoming the person she was meant to be.

Codependent adults often become addicted to alcohol, drugs, food, sex, gambling, or other things they believe will help them feel better. Because of their fear of abandonment, they also become addicted to relationships and will do anything to hold on to them. They remain in unhealthy situations far too long.

A key part of being codependent is putting aside your own wants and needs to please another person—something our culture confuses with generosity. But all it really represents is self-deception. Fearing abandonment and behaving in ways that are not true to yourself will not bring you happiness. If you are doing something for someone just to be accepted or liked, you are not being authentic—you are being manipulative. You are becoming the role you play, just as you were in your active addiction. You need to stop hiding from yourself.

Another hallmark of codependency is the need to control. In a relationship where one person is always giving and the other person is always taking, it may seem as if the taking person is in control. But that's not always the case. It's also possible to control someone by making him dependent on you for everything. You do everything for him and eventually he can't do anything for himself. He is now in a position where he can't leave you—and you are the one in control.

If that's the situation you're in, you need to stop using control as a way to cope with your fear—the same fear that led you to use drugs or drink in a destructive manner. Being at peace and aligned with the Law of Sobriety is impossible when others stay with you only out of fear or need. Happiness comes from within and from aligning your life with who you are, not from what you do or what others think of you. Your sense of self-worth increases when you feel safe and accepted for who you are, not just for what you can do for someone else.

Your expectation that people will react the way you want them to if you can just stay in control is also a losing proposition. Just as you cannot control external things, you cannot control how others respond to you. You are only in control of how *you* react and behave. If a situation or a relationship isn't working out the way you wish, remember that the only control you have is over yourself in this moment, right now.

The world around us is always changing. How often have things worked out when you thought they wouldn't? How many times did you expect the worst and it never came to pass? How much time have you spent worrying and obsessing about some situation, only to realize your worrying was just draining your energy? When you're feeling insecure and anxious, it's important to take a pause, listen to your inner voice, and let the rest go. Know that there is a master plan that will reveal itself when it is meant to—not sooner, not later.

The Law of Sobriety enables you to delight in the joys of your recovery and know you can handle the bad times without having to pick up a drink or use drugs. If you feel you are losing ground with your recovery, there is always help available. There are psychotherapists, treatment programs, twelve-step meetings, sponsors, and spiritual gurus who are always there to hold out a hand for you when you are in despair or overwhelmed. You are not in control of the universe—but you are not alone. The sooner you realize that, the more at peace you will feel.

When you give up control, you no longer need to feel like a victim. You do not need to blame anything or anyone for what you might be going through. Instead, you need to trust that your answers are out there for you. When you let go of resistance, you give up the fight against your fear and doubt; you also stop fighting against who you truly are. You open up a sacred space where the intelligence and insight of the universe has room to express itself within you. When you soften or learn to lean into your recovery (in other words, let go of your resistance to it), you allow yourself to get out of your ego. In AA they say *ego* is an acronym for "edging God out." It means that when you get caught up in your own thoughts and concerns, there is no room for the answers you seek to flow effortlessly. How can we access our spiritual nature when we are edging out our higher power?

Giving up your need for control allows you to have more compassion and tolerance for others. When you stop clinging to people, places, and things, you accept whatever comes your way in recovery: the good, the bad, and the ugly. You accept things as they are. This does not mean you are giving up. Instead, you are giving up unhealthy attachments and letting the universe take over, letting your life unfold as it should. When you do that, you are ready to engage in actions that support your purpose, your principles, and your new sober life.

There are times we need to quit torturing ourselves. Let go of what you thought would happen. If life has twisted on you, don't turn on yourself. Don't try to make things be the way they were. Come up to speed. Return to now. Let yourself accept the new situation at hand.

—From *More Language of Letting Go*
by Melody Beattie

LETTING GO OF DESIRE

When you were addicted to drugs, you used much of your energy to support your addiction—doctor shopping, panhandling for change, shoplifting, scoring drugs in dangerous parts of town, prostitution, or pawning personal items. When you could not control your drinking, you used up your energy hiding your bottles of booze from loved ones, hunting down different stores to buy your liquor, or making up excuses for why you were late or absent from work. When you let go of your old habits of using and drinking, you were able to find a new sense of freedom, weren't you? You were no longer a prisoner to your substance abuse. You finally became emotionally and physically available for those you love, as well.

We human beings are all driven by insatiable desires. When you were actively using, you would go to any lengths to feel good and would rationalize anything to avoid discomfort. You became the prisoner of your drives, rather than letting your higher power or wiser self take over during times of trouble. Contentment can only be found when you give up these self-destructive desires. Shame can only be eliminated when you begin aligning your behaviors with your morals and ideals. When you immerse yourself in your recovery, you unearth your true essence.

When you surrender to your sacred side, self-destructive behaviors are redirected toward positive solutions. That is what recovery and the Law of Sobriety are all about: taking your will out of the equation and trusting in a force larger than yourself to bring you what you need. Seeking instant gratification has not brought you the life you want. It's time to live a life that resonates from your spiritual side. When you were newly sober, that desperation to get what you wanted was still there; it just shifted to being desperate enough to do anything to remain clean and sober. The Law of Sobriety says you can put that desperation aside. Let go of doing things your way and trust in something greater than yourself to move you forward. Trust in the universe—whether you believe that's religion, mysticism, or a kind of energetic force—to get you past the suffering you have endured for so long. You will see that once you rely on these universal truths and stop resisting them, serenity and sobriety await you.

Tools for Change
A Meditation for Letting Go

One way to detach from the clinging mind is to practice a letting-go meditation.

- Close your eyes. Take in a few deep breaths and notice what it is you want to release during this meditation.
- As you let your breath out, notice what comes next. Is it release or resistance? What are you resisting? Ask yourself if it is possible to detach from what you are feeling right now.
- Notice how strong the impulse is to hang on to it. Observe the pushing and pulling of it. Watch it morph into something else. If you are still struggling, observe that.
- Ask yourself again, "Am I ready to let go?" If not, meditate on the following questions.

  ✓ What is it I am unwilling to let go of?

  ✓ What do I think I have to gain by staying attached to these feelings?

  ✓ Is this gain greater than what I will gain when I let these feelings go?

  ✓ Why am I resisting change?

  ✓ What are my fears surrounding letting it go?

  ✓ What might happen if I relinquished control right now?

  ✓ Do I trust my higher power or the universe to guide me through my recovery?

  ✓ Is my ego causing me to resist?

  ✓ Am I still attached to old belief systems that are no longer working in my recovery?

  ✓ Am I having difficulty being comfortable in the unknown?

- Once you have put these questions out to the universe, create affirmations that are designed to let go of resistance and attachments with more ease. These might include:

  ✓ I engage in my recovery process by each action step I take and not by becoming attached to the outcome.

  ✓ I am willing to let go of anything that is getting in the way of my recovery.

  ✓ I am no longer afraid of change.

  ✓ I no longer let my fears determine what I will do next in sobriety.

  ✓ If I choose to let go right now, calmness will envelop me.

  ✓ I will allow my higher power or the universe to guide me through my recovery.

  ✓ I will no longer allow my ego to edge out my spiritual growth.

  ✓ I am letting go of negative belief systems that no longer serve me.

  ✓ I am comfortable in the unknown and all the infinite possibilities that await me.

LETTING GO OF THINGS

I find my clients are sometimes unwilling to let go of their unhealthy attachments to their things, whether those things are money, prestige, house, career, or even body image. But material things come and go. When clients identify too strongly with "things" and then somehow lose them, they find themselves in my office—depressed, anxious, and sometimes even suicidal. They have completely lost themselves in these external objects. They have allowed their self-worth to be tied to these outside forces, forgetting that they are much more than the things they have lost.

I treated a man who felt trapped in his high-paying job. He was required to entertain clients in places that served alcohol, and he knew that if he continued with this company, he would not be able to stop drinking. He had to find a way out. In the course of our work together, he realized his attachment to expensive possessions and the maintenance of them was keeping him trapped financially in a job that didn't support his authentic self. He decided he could get along with fewer expensive things and use his sales talent in some other capacity that did not require entertaining with alcohol. When he let go of his attachment to his possessions, he felt relieved and was finally able to make the changes he needed to make in his life.

Sometimes, addicts and alcoholics become attached to the idea that once they obtain something, they will be able to get sober: "If only I get that promotion, I'll stop drinking" or "Once I buy that house on the lake, I'll quit using." But the promotion comes and they are still drinking; they move into that dream house and are still using. The "more" they want is never enough, because there is always a bigger house, a better job, or a more attractive partner. There is nothing wrong with wanting more, as long as you're not using what you want to numb the emptiness you have been avoiding for so long.

Otherwise, you are trading one addiction for another, expecting the next big thing to make you feel good on the inside.

LETTING GO OF SOLUTIONS

When problems arise in your life, you can teach yourself to regard them not as obstacles to be beaten down or puzzles to be solved, but as opportunities for growth and lessons to be learned. Embrace the challenges you face with an understanding that change is just around the corner. Learn to live in the unknown when you don't have an instant solution. This is another thing that makes many of us uncomfortable and requires us to let go of attachments. An answer awaits you when you learn to give up the struggle to know immediately and absolutely.

Knowing that you can only control certain aspects of your life frees you up to focus on the things you really can control. Holding on tight to the need to control people, places, and things will only keep you stuck in the vortex of pain. Show up with your complete awareness for whatever unfolds and allow your actions to come from that still place within you. When you do that, you can walk through anything. When you are willing to sit in your emotional pain and notice your thoughts ebb and flow, these experiences become less agonizing.

Your simultaneous aversion to, attachment to, and avoidance of painful thoughts are the cause of your distress. That is how fear is created. The wreckage from the past is not meant to punish you, but rather to be there as a gentle reminder of the lessons you've learned and the wisdom you've gained. Now it's time to access that wisdom.

After years and years of avoiding the trauma of their past histories, many people are suddenly immobilized with panic attacks and agonizing anxiety. That is where the danger of a relapse lies. They have never been able to let go of their attachment to their trauma.

They let it define them: "I am a woman who was abused," or "I am a man who was neglected," or "I am a child who was abandoned." Knowing that you are more than your trauma is a revelation. Learning to see your trauma mindfully with compassion takes the sting away. You do not need to stay stuck in traumatic events, nor do you need to escape from them with drugs and alcohol—or with any solution at all. You can give up your attachment to your past pain. Accept your life as it is now and freedom awaits you.

The Two Darts

"I teach suffering and the end of suffering. That is all I teach," declared the Buddha. By "suffering," he meant all forms of mental distress, such as unhappiness, disappointment, fear, and anxiety. He said real pain, both physical and mental, is part of being alive and cannot be avoided. But suffering can be. To explain this, the Buddha used the example of two darts.

He said everyone experiences real pain. When an unenlightened person experiences pain, he worries and grieves about the pain. He resists and resents it. He strives for its immediate end. It's as if such a person has been struck by two darts. The first dart is the real pain, which cannot be avoided. The second dart is all the suffering he feels at being struck by the first dart. He has pierced himself with that second dart.

The enlightened person avoids the second dart. He notices and experiences the real pain, but he does not resist or attach his thoughts to it.

The Buddha also said the only way an unenlightened person knows how to escape the pain of the second dart is by seeking pleasure. He becomes attached to pleasure and afraid of pain. But it is this attachment to pleasure that brings him pain. If he was not attached to pleasure—if he could simply accept the unavoidable pain of the first dart—he would never be pierced with the second dart. So, paradoxically, the attachment to pleasure inevitably brings us more pain—pain that can be avoided.

The next time you catch yourself resisting and resenting your pain, just remind yourself, "Take out the second dart."

RESISTING WHO YOU REALLY ARE

When you resist who you are, you are not accepting life on its own terms. When you are pushing against the flow of life, you are telling the universe that it is wrong. You are demanding the universe do it your way. How could you ever hope to succeed? The problem with resisting the universe is that you will attract back nothing but resistance. Remember, this is how the Law of Sobriety works.

When you are resentful, angry, and frustrated at the way things are, you are resonating negative emotions. Those negative emotions put you in a negative mind-set, and harmful behaviors will follow. Instead, if you trust the universe, you resonate positive emotions, and thus, positive energy will flow back to you. You feel alive and energetic, able to follow your recovery plan. Activities such as going to a twelve-step meeting, talking to a sponsor, attending a spiritual retreat, meditating, repeating your intentions, going to a therapy session, or practicing yoga will be effortless.

Just by accepting what "is" and giving up the struggle of what "should be," you begin to live on purpose and in alignment with your truest essence. You take self-centeredness and ego out of the equation and let the Law of Sobriety work in your life. You let the universe do its job. Your recovery no longer feels like an endless obligation, but instead it becomes an expression of your truest desires to live clean and sober. You become more willing to embrace your recovery when you let go of your resistance to who you are and how things "should be." You have more patience to do what is required to stay clean and sober. You realize that the actions you take today will affect tomorrow and every day thereafter.

Tools for Change
Exercises in Letting Go

- *Letting go of people you are attached to or addicted to or codependent with.* Imagine you are ensnared in a net that is attached to, the other party. See yourself with a pair of scissors, cutting yourself free! Then see yourself standing free without any attachments to the other party. Spin around once, swinging your arms around you to relish your freedom.

- *Letting go of your attachment to things.* Start by taking one thing that you are attached to, that "owns you," and give it away permanently. Make a list of everything else that "owns you." Bless each item on your list and release your emotional attachment to it. Imagine what life will be like with nothing that requires your maintenance, care, money to buy or sustain it, or time to keep it. Imagine being stress free because you have no attachments and responsibilities—only the time and freedom to live and do noble activities that bring you closer to who you are at your core; to celebrate living, loving, giving, and serving.

- *Letting go of your attachment to negative, harmful memories.* Buy a metal box. Imagine this box is so strong, leakproof, and reinforced that it can forever contain anything placed in it. Place those memories that you are so attached to, that permeate, terrorize, and paralyze your life, into this box. Write a full description on paper of the contents and put it in the box. Then take the box to the local waste dump and dispose of it. There! You're done with those memory attachments, and you are free to start over and live life with a clean slate.

- *Letting go of your attachment to harmful emotions.* Make a list of every emotion that makes you feel contracted or restricted on a regular basis—the harmful emotions that you feel control you, that take over your life. Now go get a big, flat rock for each one and write that emotion on the rock in paint or felt pen. Take all your rocks down to the nearest large body of water and drop those heavy rocks into the water, one by one. You're releasing that emotion to the depths, and you are freeing your life of these heavy rocks that were weighing you down.

This exercise was written by and is used with permission from Jackie Lapin, author of The Art of Conscious Creation: How You Can Transform the World, *who guides you on how to consciously create your life and become a better, faster manifestor. For books, tools, and daily manifesting tips, go to www.theartofconscious creation.com.*

Conclusion

Sobriety is all about being aware of and accepting all your in-securities, fears, guilt, and all the other parts of yourself that you see as flaws. It's about having the trust to turn over unhealthy percep-tions to spiritual growth. To have that psychic shift, you must be will-ing to trust and turn over these imperfections to something greater than yourself—whether you call that something God, Buddha, Allah, a higher power, or universal energy. You must be willing to release all the toxic energy your negative thought patterns create and replace them with thoughts that match your true resonance. Your destiny is determined by how you consciously expend your energies. And this, of course, means your destiny is in your own hands.

Are you letting go of negative thought patterns? Do you trust your innate wisdom? Are you letting go of self-deprecating belief systems? Are you judging yourself and others harshly, or are you forgiving yourself and them for any shortcomings? Are you enlisting the sup-port of others to help you through this process? Are you allowing past traumas to get in the way of your future successes, or are you em-bracing them as opportunities for growth?

When you begin to dig deep into your soul for the answers to these questions, you open up an enormous opportunity to transform your-self and your life. If you start believing, "Yes, I can do this," even when everyone else is saying, "No you can't," you will be surprised how empowered you can feel. The opportunities are endless, personally and professionally, when you stop judging yourself so harshly. You have the power right now to change things, even if it feels uncom-fortable. Tremendous growth can be achieved when you walk through your fears and become who you were always intended to be.

If you are sober but are letting your character defects run the show, you are abandoning your true self. If you are putting others down to lift yourself up, you may feel better temporarily, but the damage you cause will only come back to harm you and may even cause you to relapse. When you don't ask others for help, you run the risk of allowing your ego to direct your actions. When your ego is in charge, spirituality cannot emerge. Spiritual emptiness leads you to drift away from your true essence. When you don't live in truth, you may seek temporary means to numb the pain of not being authentic. And that is when you run the risk of falling back into old destructive, compulsive patterns.

Finally, remember that maintaining sobriety is a process. You have to walk the path, knowing that the Law of Sobriety is your guide to a joyous recovery. When you are in balance and in the flow, you will feel it. When you relinquish all the grasping and attachment to what recovery should feel like, you will finally be free to be sober. You will not need to obsess anymore about what lies ahead. You will be able to sit back and enjoy the ride by letting the universe handle the particulars and using the Law of Sobriety as your road map.

Life, life, life. It is better the second time around, for when you awake in consciousness, doubt and fear evaporate; there is nothing to sustain them. Come out and greet the life for which you have been ready and reaching.

—From *Be Still and Know*
by Mara Marin

My hope for you is that in your recovery, you find a path that is as unique as you are. Recovery is not meant to be "one size fits all." As you embrace the seven steps of the Law of Sobriety, know that they need not be accomplished in any order. Find the order that works for your healing process.

If embracing mindfulness—being in those moments of complete and utter presence—helps you access your higher power, start there.

If you are learning to act rather than react by living a life of right action, start your recovery process there.

If in the still moments of meditation you gain clarity as to what your life purpose is, begin there.

If letting go of years of shame that has enslaved you opens up a doorway to your true self, start there.

If the layers of your false self unravel as you identify your authentic self, begin there.

If living a life of value brings you compassion and forgiveness for yourself and others, start there.

And if forgiving yourself brings you peace and tranquillity, begin there.

Just as there is not one road to recovery, there is not one way to work through the steps of the Law of Sobriety. I trust that if you just begin somewhere, there will be an innate knowing of what comes next. However, if you are the type of person who needs a set plan, then following the steps as they are presented in this book may be right for you. Just remember not to judge yourself, no matter where you start and what progress you make. Give yourself the same compassion you would offer another person in recovery. There is no right way to go through this process. The best way is to go through it one day at a time and, if need be, one minute at a time. You can always start anew if you get off track. Every beginning is a moment of hope.

A life lived with purpose and meaning is much more fulfilling than just remaining clean and sober but discontent. It is about finding a journey of recovery that allows you to be the person you were always meant to be. You are not your disease and never were. Your disease is not the only thing that defines you; it is an aspect of your actions that you can change.

I believe a life filled with joy and serenity awaits you in all areas of your life.

If your desire is to be in a loving relationship, add that to your recovery plan.

If you have always wanted to quit that nine-to-five job to become a novelist, start writing.

If learning how to be a salsa dancer has always been a desire, sign up for a class.

If climbing the Himalayas and taking up kundalini yoga sound enticing, start climbing and stretching.

If staying home and making banana bread sounds appealing, start baking.

There is never a perfect time in your recovery to fulfill your greatest passions. But it is equally true that there is never a better time to begin than *right now*. All you need is a desire, a plan, and a willingness to live your greatest life. Get started.

Resources

Here are some books, websites, and CDs that will help you learn more about the practices presented in this book.

WEBSITES

ABC of Yoga
www.abc-of-yoga.com
Learn about every aspect of yoga, from breathing techniques, to postures, to health benefits. There is also a forum to share information and ideas.

Alcoholics Anonymous
www.aa.org
This site has many articles about what AA is and how twelve-step meetings work. You can also use it to find a meeting in your area.

BeliefNet
www.beliefnet.com
This site contains information about almost thirty different faiths, as well asnondenominational spirituality. There are sections on prayer, inspiration, health, holistic living, love and family, and more. Influential people in various fields maintain blogs here, including Sherry Gaba, LCSW.

The Chopra Center
www.chopra.com/library?gclid=CMOnrsr43Z0CFdFL5Qod1V_kLg
This section of the Chopra Center website contains several guided visualizations that you can listen to on your computer.

Dharma Seed
www.dharmaseed.org
Dharma Seed is dedicated to preserving the teachings of a branch of Buddhism that cultivates wisdom and insight. The site offers a

wide selection of free streaming lectures by meditation and mindfulness teachers.

Find-a-Therapist
www.find-a-therapist.com
This is a therapist directory. You can search for a therapist by region and type of practice. The site also includes helpful articles written by therapists on a wide variety of topics.

Guided Visualization
video.google.com/videoplay?docid=-8845129782533837583#
You'll find a nine-minute guided visualization, with images, here.

Inquiring Mind
www.inquiringmind.com
Inquiring Mind is an online journal about the philosophy and ideas of Buddhism. Many of the contributors are not Buddhists, but write about mindfulness and mindful living.

Journal for You
www.journalforyou.com
This site offers articles about different ways to start journaling, interviews with journaling experts, reviews of journal technique books, historical and private journals, a hints and tips section, and many useful links to other journaling sites.

Mind Tools
www.mindtools.com
This site provides a wide array of tools to help advance your career, but the skills it discusses are also good life management tools. They include problem solving, stress management, decision making, time management, communication skills, and memory improvement.

Narcotics Anonymous
www.na.org
This site has many articles about what NA is and the services it offers. You can also use it to find a meeting in your area.

The Positive Psychology Center at the University of Pennsylvania
www.positivepsychology.org
This site has resources to learn more about positive psychology, including articles and videos about research findings. It also has a link to the Positive Psychology Center's Authentic Happiness website, which includes questionnaires and studies that will help you learn more about yourself.

Sounds True
www.soundstrue.com
This online store offers audio and DVD presentations, podcasts, books, and online courses by well-known experts in areas that include guided visualization, meditation, mindfulness, psychology, yoga, Buddhism, health, healing, and spirituality.

Vital Affirmations
www.vitalaffirmations.com
This website is dedicated to tools that help cultivate a positive mindset. It includes many positive affirmations and advice about how to use them to effect positive change in your life. It also has articles about journaling, meditation, conscious living, and gratitude.

Wellness and Recovery
www.wellnessandrecovery.com
This website provides a wealth of information for anyone seeking to enhance their recovery through embracing a healthy lifestyle. Topics covered include nutritional foundations for recovery, fitness and recovery, conquering nicotine addiction, pursuing your central purpose in life, and more.

GUIDED MEDITATION CDS

Kabat-Zinn, Jon. *Mindfulness for Beginners: Explore the Infinite Potential that Lies Within This Very Moment.* Sounds True, 2006.

Kornfield, Jack. *Guided Meditation: Six Essential Practices to Cultivate Love, Awareness, and Wisdom.* Sounds True, 2007.

Reis, Jennifer. *Guided Relaxation: Yoga Nidra.* Jennifer Reis, 2006.

SUGGESTED READING

Adams, Kathleen. *Journal to the Self: Twenty-two Paths to Personal Growth.* Grand Central, 1990.

Begley, Sharon. *Train Your Mind, Change Your Brain: How a New Science Reveals Our Extraordinary Potential to Transform Ourselves.* Ballantine Books, 2007.

Brach, Tara, Ph.D. *Radical Acceptance: Embracing Your Life with the Heart of a Buddha.* Bantam Books, 2004.

DeSalvo, Louise. *Writing as a Way of Healing: How Telling Our Stories Transforms Our Lives.* Beacon, 2000.

Doland, Erin R. *Unclutter Your Life in One Week.* Simon Spotlight Entertainment, 2009.

Gawain, Shakti. *Creative Visualization: Use the Power of Your Imagination to Create What You Want in Your Life.* Nataraj, 2002.

Grabhorn, Lynn. *Excuse Me, Your Life Is Waiting: The Astonishing Power of Feelings.* Hampton Roads, 2003.

Kabat-Zinn, Jon. *Wherever You Go, There You Are.* Hyperion, 1994.

Pennebaker, James, Ph.D. *Opening Up: The Healing Power of Expressing Emotions.* Guilford Publications, 1997.

Rosenberg, Larry. *Breath by Breath: The Liberating Practice of Insight Meditation.* Shambhala Publications, 2004.

Rossman, Martin, M.D. *Guided Imagery for Self-Healing.* Starseed Press, 2000.

Seligman, Martin E. P., Ph.D. *Learned Optimism: How to Change Your Mind and Your Life.* Knopf Doubleday, 2006.

Sisgold, Steve. *What's Your Body Telling You? Listening to Your Body's Signals to Stop Anxiety, Erase Self-Doubt, and Achieve True Wellness.* McGraw-Hill, 2009.

Selected References

Brown, R., M.D., and P. Gerbarg, M.D. "Sudarshan Kriya yogic breathing in the treatment of stress, anxiety, and depression: Part I—Neurophysiologic model." *Journal of Alternative and Complimentary Medicine* 11, no. 1 (February 2005).

Brown, R., M.D., and P. Gerbarg, M.D. "Sudarshan Kriya yogic breathing in the treatment of stress, anxiety, and depression: Part II—Clinical applications and guidelines." *Journal of Alternative and Complimentary Medicine* 11, no. 4 (August 2005).

Brownlow, Sheila and Renee D. Reasinger. "Putting off until tomorrow what is better done today: Academic procrastination as a function of motivation toward college work." *Journal of Social Behavior & Personality* 15, no. 5 (Special Issue, 2000).

Burns, David D., M.D. *The Feeling Good Handbook.* William Morrow and Company, 1989.

Dayton, T., Ph.D. "What about the family? The adult children of alcoholics' co-dependent story." Scriptamus, November 18, 2009. Accessed at http://scriptamus.wordpress.com.

Dewitte, Siegfried and Henri C. Schouwenburg. "Procrastination, temptations, and incentives: the struggle between the present and the future in procrastinators and the punctual." *European Journal of Personality* 16, no. 6 (November/December 2002).

Freud, Sigmund. "Beyond the Pleasure Principle." 1920.

Harvard Women's Health Watch 11, no. 6 (February 2004).

Harlow, Lisa L., Michael D. Newcomb, and P. M. Bentler. "Depression, self-derogation, substance use, and suicide ideation: Lack of purpose in life as a mediational factor." *Journal of Clinical Psychology* 42, no. 1 (February 2006).

Horney, K. *Neurosis and Human Growth.* W. W. Norton, 1950.

Husén, T., and T. Neville Postlethwaite, eds. *The International Encyclopedia of Education.* Elsevier Science, 1994.

Luskin, F., Ph.D. "Stanford Forgiveness Projects—Research Applications." Stanford University Center for Research in Disease Prevention. *Proceedings from the Conference on Scientific Findings About Forgiveness,* October 2003.

Lutz, A., J. Brefczynski-Lewis, T. Johnstone, and R. J. Davidson. "Regulation of the neural circuitry of emotion by compassion meditation: Effects of meditative expertise." *Public Library of Science One* 3, no. 3 (March 26, 2008).

MacLean, C. R. K., K. G. Walton, S. R. Wenneberg, D. K. Levitsky, J. P. Mandarino, R. Waziri, S. L. Hillis, and R. H. Schneider. "Effects of the transcendental meditation program on adaptive mechanisms: Changes in hormone levels and responses to stress after 4 months of practice." *Psychoneuroendocrinology* 22, no. 4 (May 1997).

Maselko, J., Sc.D. "Forgiveness is associated with psychological health, findings from the General Social Survey." Harvard School of Public Health. *Proceedings from the Conference on Scientific Findings About Forgiveness,* October 2003.

Moore, A., and P. Malinowski. "Meditation, mindfulness and cognitive flexibility." *Consciousness and Cognition* 18, no. 1 (March 2009).

Peterson, C., Ph.D., and M. E. P. Seligman, Ph.D. *Character Strengths and Virtues: A Handbook and Classification.* Oxford University Press, 2004.

Pace, T. W. W., L. T. Negi, D. D. Adame, S. P. Cole, T. I. Sivilli, T. D. Brown, M. J. Issa, and C. L. Raison. "Compassion meditation may improve physical and emotional responses to psychological stress." *Psychoneuroendocrinology* 34, no. 1 (January 2009).

Salloum, J. B., V. A. Ramchandani, J. Bodurka, R. Rawlings, D. George, and D. W. Hommer. "Blunted rostral anterior cingulated response during a simplified decoding task of negative emotional facial expressions in alcoholic patients." *Alcoholism: Clinical and Experimental Research* 31, no. 9 (2007): 1490–1504.

Seligman, M. E. P., T. A. Steen, N. Park, and C. Peterson. "Positive psychology progress: Empirical validation of interventions." *American Psychologist* 60, no. 5 (July–August 2005).

Seligman, M. E. P., T. Rashid, and A. C. Parks. "Positive Psychotherapy." *American Psychologist* 61, no. 8 (November 2006).

Sudsuang, R., V. Chentanez, and K. Veluvan. "Effect of Buddhist meditation on serum cortisol and total protein levels, blood pressure, pulse rate, lung volume and reaction time." *Physiology and Behavior* 50, no. 3 (September 1991).

Tice, Dianne M. and Roy F. Baumeister. "Longitudinal study of procrastination, performance, stress, and health: The costs and benefits of dawdling." *Psychological Science* 8, no. 6 (November 1977).

Tiebout, H. M., M.D. "Therapeutic mechanisms of Alcoholics Anonymous." *American Journa.l of Psychiatry* no. 100 (January 1944).

University of Massachusetts Medical School, Center for Mindfulness in Medicine, Health Care, and Society. Accessed at www.umassmed.edu/cfm/.

Index

About the Authors

Sherry Gaba, LCSW, is an experienced professional in the field of addictions and recovery. A licensed psychotherapist and life coach who attended the famous Coaches Training Institute, Sherry received her Master of Social Work from the prestigious University of Southern California. With fifteen years of experience as a clinician, she has also worked at some of the top rehab centers including the famed Promises Treatment Center in Malibu, California. The success of her private practice and coaching program made her the go-to expert for Dr. Drew Pinsky on VH1's *Celebrity Rehab 2* and its spinoff, *Sober House,* and she appeared as the Life Coach on *Celebrity Rehab 3* in spring 2010. Sherry's expertise has been quoted in *Cosmopolitan, New York Daily News,* E! Online, and Elle.com, and she has appeared on *Issues with Jane Velez-Mitchell, Hollywood Confidential, Inside Edition, Dr. Drew Live,* Fox News in San Diego, and KTLA-TV in Los Angeles. Sherry is a frequent contributor to anthologies, blogs, and newsletters, is a sought-after speaker, and lives with her family in Southern California where she maintains an active private practice. Visit Sherry at www.sgabatherapy.com for information about life-coaching programs, teleseminars, and webinars, and read her blogs at CounselorMagazine.com and BeliefNet.com.

Beth Adelman has been working as a writer, journalist, and editor for twenty-five years. She has written three books for adults, seven children's books, and countless magazine, newspaper, and web articles. Beth also works with corporate clients to help them present and refine their unique message. Her work has covered a very wide variety of topics, including science, medicine, history, sports, the arts, and animals.